Junior NKIERE MAKOLONI

COMPUTER COURSES SECOND YEAR SA

Junior NKIERE MAKOLONI

COMPUTER COURSES SECOND YEAR SA

ScienciaScripts

Imprint
Any brand names and product names mentioned in this book are subject to trademark, brand or patent protection and are trademarks or registered trademarks of their respective holders. The use of brand names, product names, common names, trade names, product descriptions etc. even without a particular marking in this work is in no way to be construed to mean that such names may be regarded as unrestricted in respect of trademark and brand protection legislation and could thus be used by anyone.

Cover image: www.ingimage.com

This book is a translation from the original published under ISBN 978-620-6-71552-8.

Publisher:
Sciencia Scripts
is a trademark of
Dodo Books Indian Ocean Ltd. and OmniScriptum S.R.L publishing group

120 High Road, East Finchley, London, N2 9ED, United Kingdom
Str. Armeneasca 28/1, office 1, Chisinau MD-2012, Republic of Moldova, Europe
Managing Directors: Ieva Konstantinova, Victoria Ursu
info@omniscriptum.com

Printed at: see last page
ISBN: 978-620-8-51188-3

Contents

PREFACE

Today's world is evolving at the pace of computers and the Internet (information highways). All aspects of our society are governed by an organisation and administration based on information technology. Information technology, which has until now been considered and used as a tool and support for certain subjects in national education systems, must become a real subject of study in its own right. And this teaching can only be done effectively on the basis of a well-written support by an IT specialist, while respecting the country's national curriculum.

In particular, the teaching of this course will lead the student to adopt responsible behaviour and demonstrate practical life skills in relation to IT.

We would like to thank the Ministere Provincial de l'EPST Haut-Uele and the Inspection Principale Provincial de Haut-Uele 2 for their involvement in the production of this book, which will be of use not only to the Province of Haut-Uele but also to all the schools in our country that offer the Secretariat-Administration option.

We recommend that schools understand the usefulness of IT tools and that they do more to unlock the mysteries of this new subject, which will turn Congolese children into responsible individuals who are useful to themselves and to society.

SUMMARY

The second year of the Secretariat-Administration humanities is largely based on IT concepts geared towards the execution of procedures relating to the processing of a file, information processing and report drafting, daily prioritisation of work to be carried out, planning meetings, staff travel and trips, mastery of basic IT concepts, use of the internet and drawing up a document.

The IT sector attracts a large number of people who are looking for career guidance or retraining, because of the wealth and diversity of career opportunities it offers. The sector is constantly evolving, with plenty of scope for innovation and career opportunities. However, students need to be aware of the various disadvantages associated with this sector.

As we said in the previous book on the first year of the Secretariat-Administration humanities, the aim of secondary education is to provide pupils with general and specific knowledge to enable them to understand the elements of the national and international cultural heritage. It also aims to develop critical thinking, creativity and intellectual curiosity, and to prepare students for a trade or profession, or for the pursuit of higher or university studies.

The drafting of a book is a vital necessity in order to remedy the many problems and challenges, such as the failure to respect the national curriculum for computer courses for some and the partial respect of this national curriculum for others, which proves a lack of professionalism in teaching, because the ultimate aim of national education is the harmonious formation of the Congolese person, a responsible citizen, useful to himself and to society, capable of promoting the development of the country and national culture, (Loi-cadre n°86-005 du 22 /09/1986 de l'Enseignement National) L'ecole doit donc former des citoyens producteurs, créatifs, cultives, consciencieux, libres et responsables, ouverts aux valeurs sociales, culturelles et esthetiques, spirituelles et republicaines (Charte de l'Education, CNS, 1992).

The second-year student who has successfully completed this course will be able to practise all the above for our purposes and manipulate the various operating (Windows) and application programmes (Internet Explorer Web browser, Basic language, Microsoft Word word processor and Microsoft Excel spreadsheet).

OBJECTIVE

GENERAL OBJECTIVE

By the end of the second year of the secretarial-administrative humanities course, the learner will be able to put an office in order, enter text correctly and carry out operations in Excel.

SPECIFIC OBJECTIVES

At the end of the second year of the Humanities Secretariat-Administration, any student who has followed the IT course assiduously will be able to :

1. Carry out the procedures involved in processing a case;
2. Process reformation and draw up a report;
3. Hierarchise the work to be carried out on a daily basis;
4. Planning staff meetings, travel and trips;
5. Explain the basic concepts of computing;
6. Using the Internet ;
7. Using the keyboard and mouse ;
8. Drawing up a document.

REMINDER: ORGANISATION OF INFORMATION

EXERCISES: See Year [1] exercises on files, document records, Excel spreadsheets, PowerPoint presentations, file organisation, file management, ...

CHAPTER I

LIBRARY MANAGEMENT

I.1.CREATION OF A LIBRARY

I.1.1.DEFINITION

A **digital** (virtual or online or electronic) **library** is a collection of **digital** (i.e. digitised or born **digital**) documents (text, images, sound) that can be accessed remotely (in particular via the Internet), offering different ways of accessing information for the public.

Method 1 :

1. Press Windows + E to open File Explorer and click on Libraries.
2. Right-click on an empty area of the Libraries window, click on New, then on Library.
3. Name the new library and include/add folders to the new library.

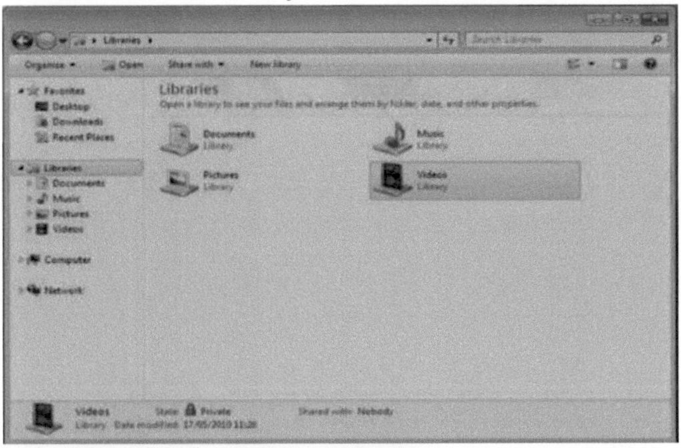

I.1.2.CREATING A NEW LIBRARY

You can easily create your own personalised libraries.

1. To create a new library, **Travail** for example, return to the **Libraries** folder.

2. Click on the **New library** button.

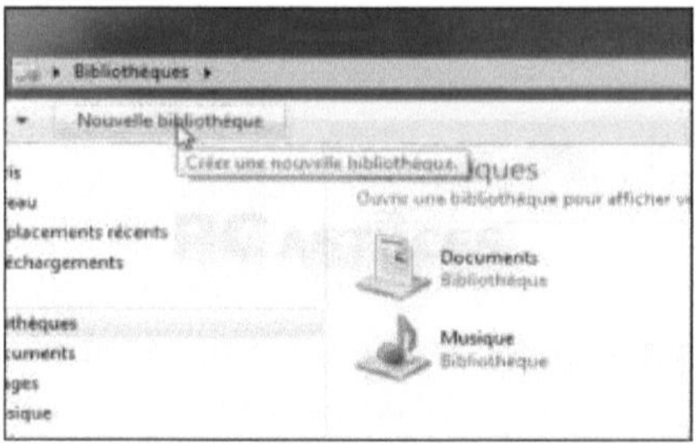

3. Give it a name and double-click to open it.

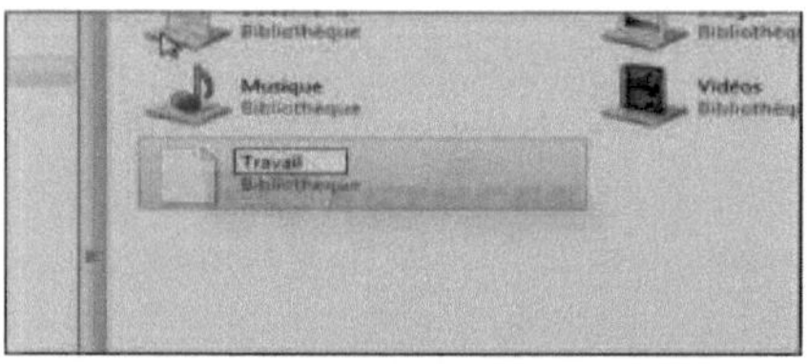

4. Then click on the **Include a folder** button.

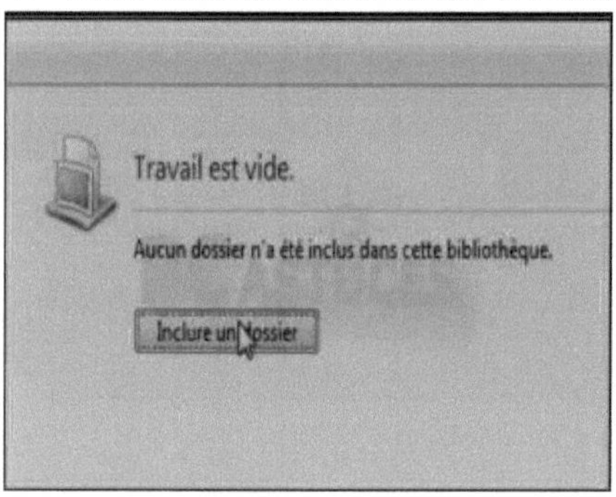

5. Select a folder on your hard drive to reference in this library and click **Include folder**.

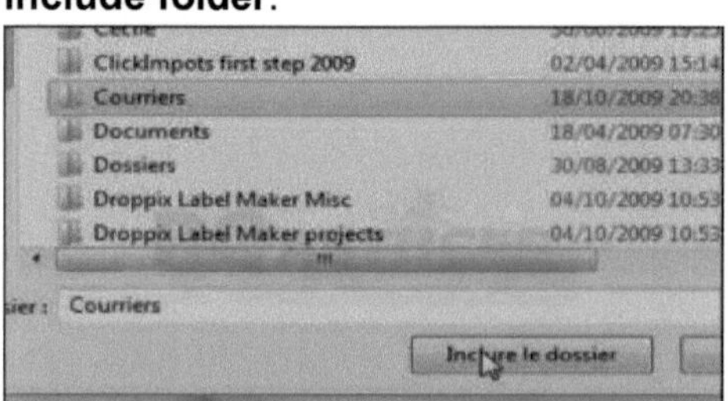

6. The folder and its contents can then be accessed from the library

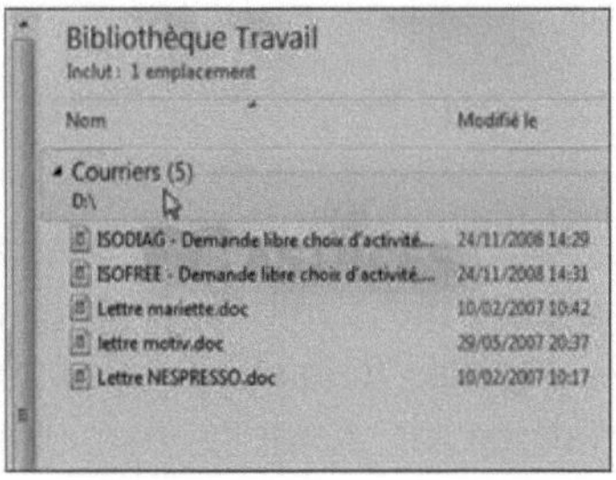

To delete a library, right-click on it and choose the **Delete** command. Note that deleting a library does not delete the files it contained. They remain in their original locations

I.2.METHODS FOR FINDING A DOCUMENT IN A FILE

To search for your files in Windows 10, use one of the following methods:

1. From the taskbar

Type the name of a document (or a keyword in it) in the search box in the taskbar. You'll see the results for the documents on your PC and OneDrive under **Best results**.

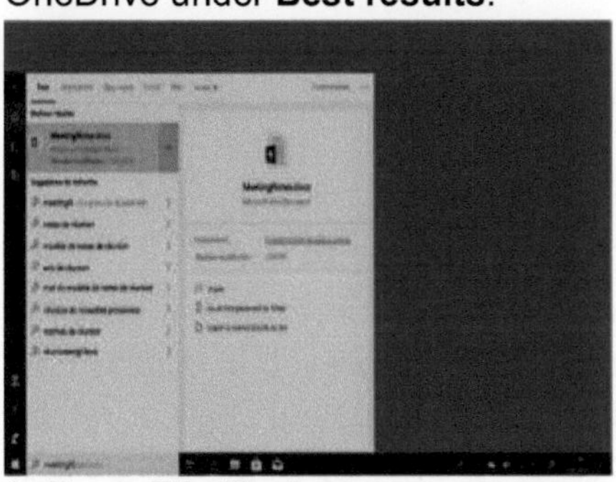

2. From File Explorer

Open **File Explorer** from the taskbar or right-click on the **Start** menu, choose **File Explorer**, then select a location in the left pane to search or browse. For example, select **This PC** to search all the devices and drives on your computer, or select **Documents** to search only the files stored there.

CHAPTER II

EXCEL

II.1.GRAPHICS

Excel offers a wide range of charts with very detailed options. The aim is to be able to represent data visually, whatever the context. A **graph** makes it easier to read and interpret the results. It can be used to highlight remarkable points, highlight variations or instantly highlight problems that need to be corrected.

II.1.1.GRAPHIC SHEET AND GRAPHIC OBJECT

Graphs can be used to display series of numerical data in graphic form to make it easier to understand large quantities of data and the relationship between different series of data.

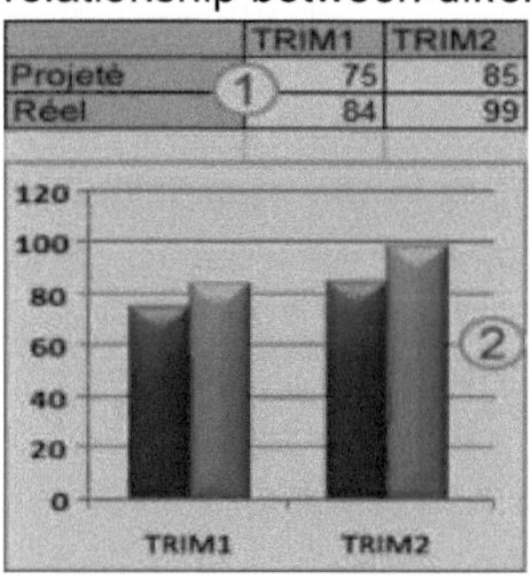

1. Spreadsheet data
2. Graph created from spreadsheet data

Excel supports many different types of chart to allow you to display data in a way that makes it easy to read. When you create a chart or modify an existing one, you can choose from many chart types (a histogram or pie chart, for example) and their sub-types (a stacked histogram or 3D pie chart, for example). You can also create a combined chart by creating a chart that uses several chart types.

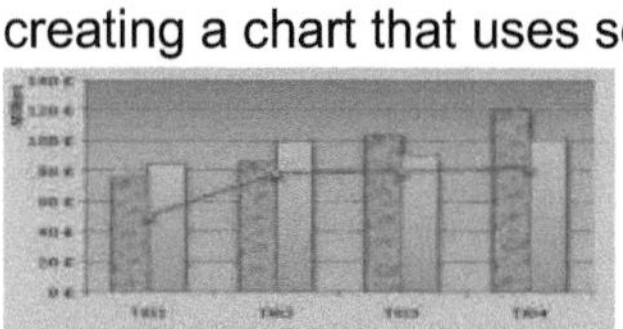

II.1.2 CREATING A GRAPH

1. OPEN EXCEL DOCUMENT

To begin, open the Excel file containing the data you want to illustrate with graphs. In this example, the owner of a restaurant wants to present the restaurant's 2019 activity report to his employees in order to make them aware of certain realities in the most eloquent way possible. His data table is as follows:

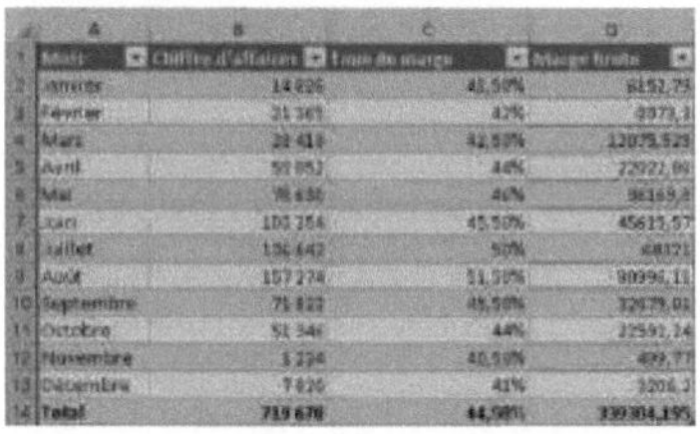

A quick analysis of the figures shows that the business is strongly affected by seasonality, with a high level of sales in the summer months, and very few visitors during the rest of the year. What's more, the margin rate seems to fall sharply in the months when business is weakest. It is precisely around these two aspects that the restaurateur would like to structure his presentation.

2. SELECT THE DATA CONCERNED

Once your data collection is open, select the table columns containing the data required for your graph. Here, to illustrate the extent of the phenomenon of seasonality, the restaurant owner selects the first two columns of his table (without taking the last row of totals).

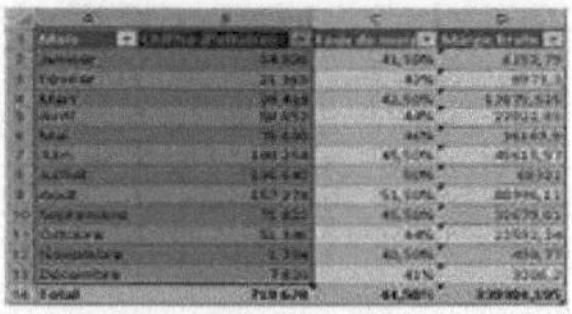

3. CHOOSE THE TYPE OF CHART

Then simply indicate the type of chart you wish to create. To do this, in the **Insert** tab, click on **Recommended Charts** to choose from Excel's suggested charts, or open one of the drop-down lists available in the **Charts** group, then select the chart model you want.

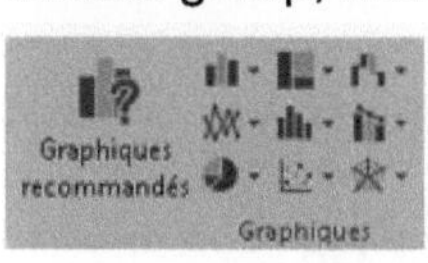

In this example, the restorer scrolls down the **Insert a curve or area chart** list and selects the first option available in the **2D Curve** models.

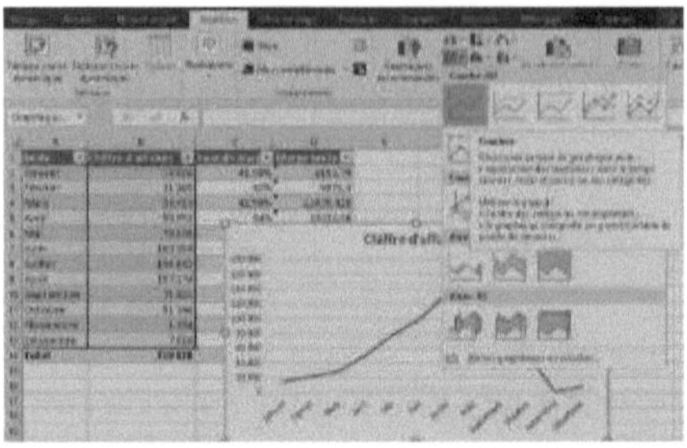

The curve obtained clearly highlights the strong seasonal nature of the restaurant's frequentation.

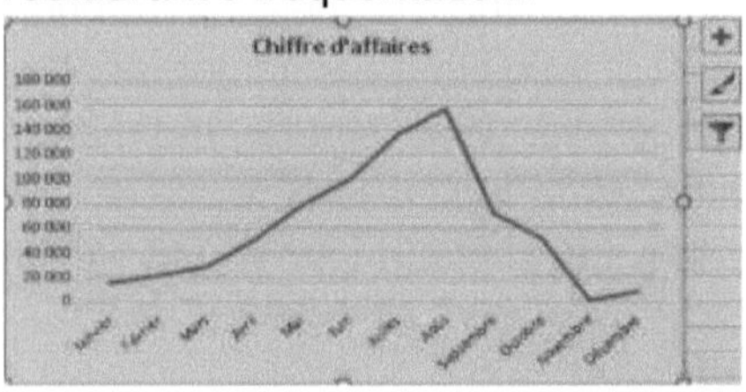

11.1.3. MODIFYING A GRAPHIC

To modify a graph ;

Right-click on your **graph**, then select Select data. In the Legend (Series) box, click on the series you want to **change**. Click on **Modify**, make the desired changes, then click on OK.

Or

a) Right-click on your graph, then **select Select data.**

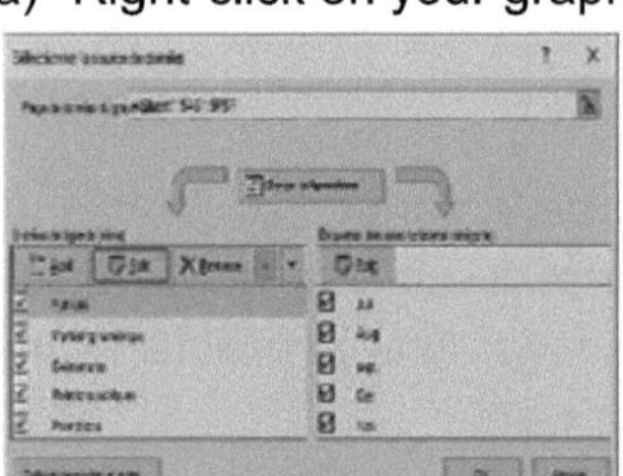

b) In the **Legend entry (Series)** area, click on the series you want to modify.

c) Click **Modify**, make the changes you want, then click **OK**.

NB: The changes you make may interrupt the links with the data source on the spreadsheet.

d) To reorganise a series, select it, then click on

Move **towards** the **LLou** Move towards the

11.1.4. AXIS TITLE

a) Adding axis titles

Select your chart, then access the Chart Design tab which appears. Click on the arrow for the drop-down menu **Add Chart Element** Move the cursor over **Axis Titles**. In the pop-up window, select "**Primary Horizontal or Primary Vertical** or both.

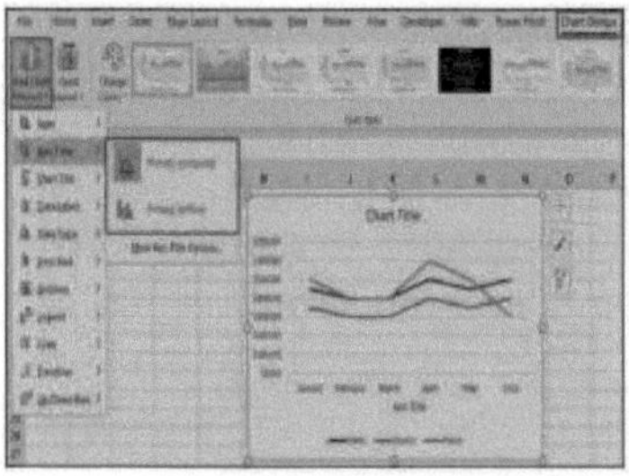

If you are using Excel on Windows, you can also use the chart elements icon to the right of the chart. Tick the box for axis titles, click on the arrow to the right, then tick the boxes for horizontal, vertical or both.

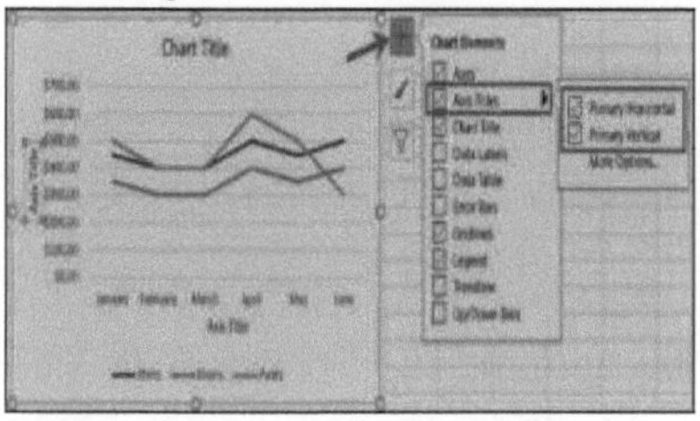

When the title of the axis you select appears on the graph, it has a default name for the axis title. Select the text box containing the default title and add your own.

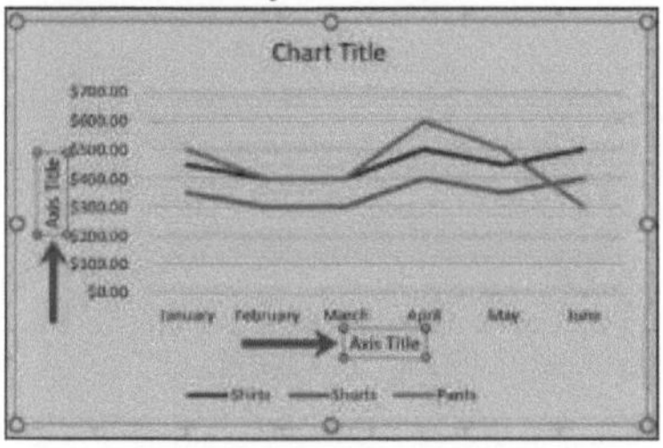

b) Customise the titles of the axes on the graph

You can customise both the title zones of the axes and the text inside these zones. And there are several ways of doing this.

First of all, right-click on the axis title to display the floating toolbar. You will see the Style, Fill and Outline options.

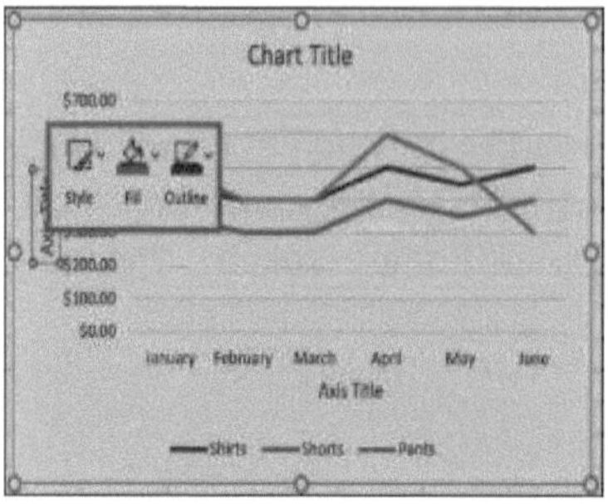

Use the drop-down arrows next to one of these options to apply a theme, use a gradient or texture, or choose a border style and colour.

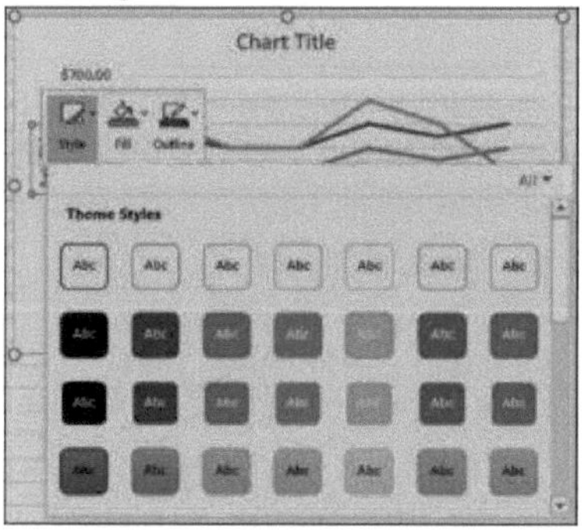

To increase customisation a little, start by opening the Format Axis Title sidebar. You can either right-click on an address and select "**Axis address formatOr** double-click
on an address.

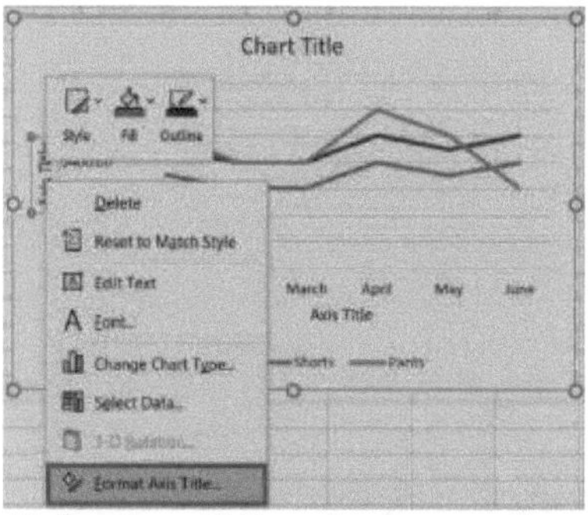

At the top of the sidebar, make sure you see the title options. Then use the three tabs just below for Fill & Line, Effects and Size & Properties to make your adjustments.

You can do things like change the fill or outline, add a shadow or glow, or adjust the alignment.

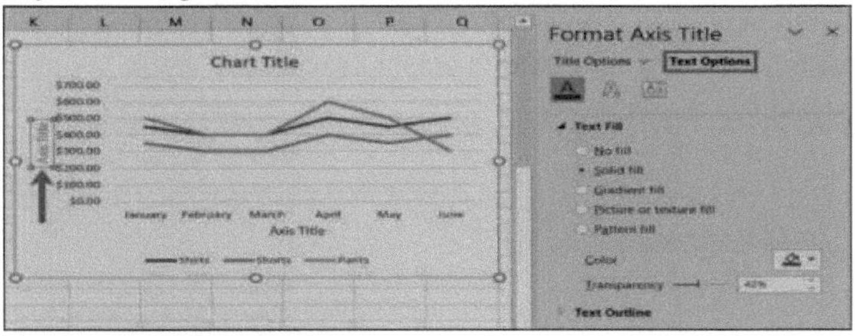

c) To customise the font

Select Text Options at the top of the sidebar. Then use the tabs for text fill, outline, text effects and text area.

You can then do things like change the colour or transparency of the font, use an XNUMXD format or change the direction of the text.

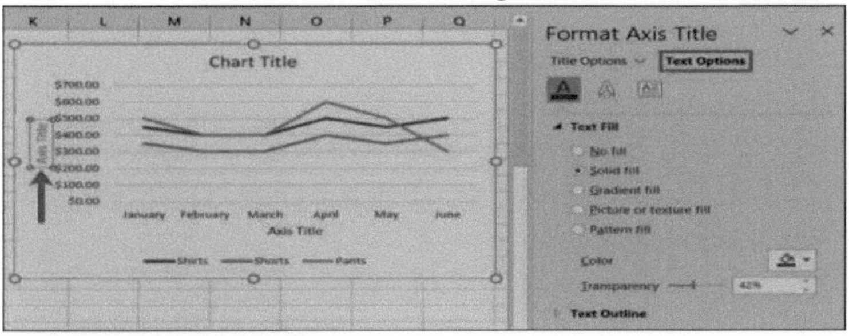

d) Delete chart axis titles

If you decide later to delete one or both of the axis titles, it will be just as easy to add them.

Select the chart and access the Chart Design tab. Click on the Add Chart Element drop-down arrow, move the cursor over the axis titles and deselect "Primary Horizontal", "Primary Vertical" or both.

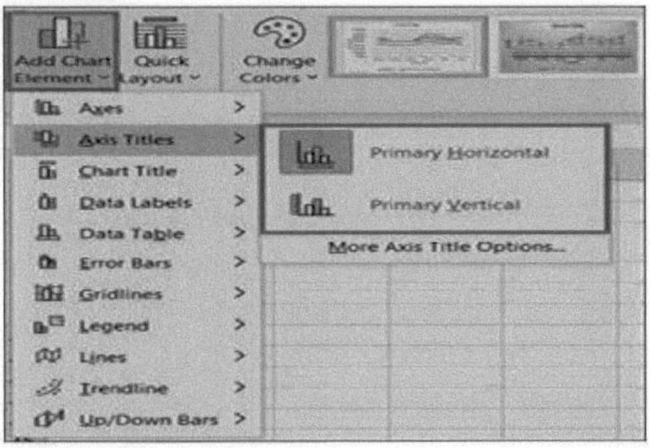

In Excel under Windows, you can also click on the chart elements icon and uncheck the axis titles box to delete both. If you want to keep a title, use the arrow next to the axis titles and select the one you want.

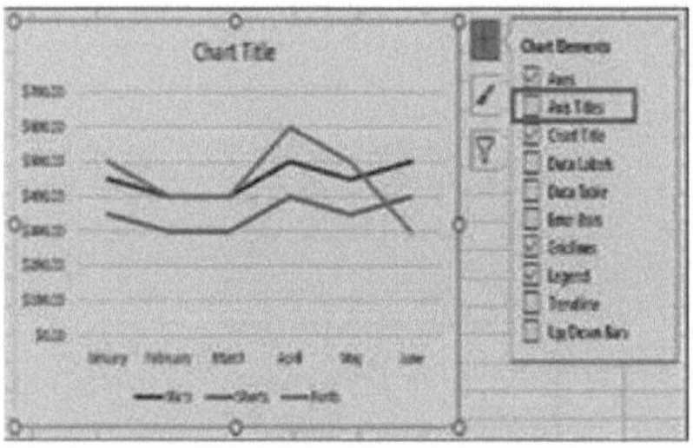

11.1.5. LEGEND

To legend a graph in Excel ;

1. **Click on the chart** to which you want to add a legend, click on the **Chart elements + button, then click on Legend.**

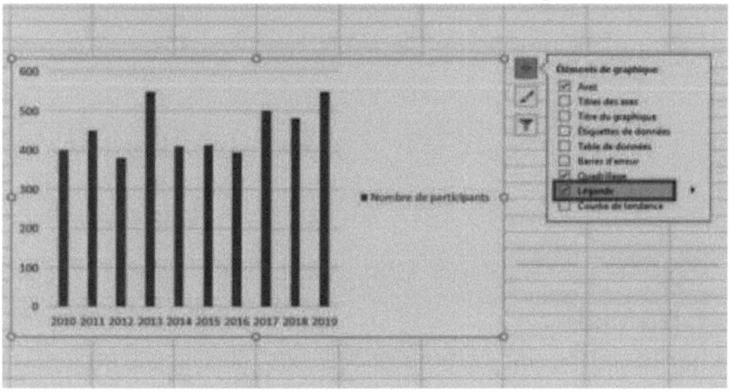

3. To change the position of the legend, click **on the arrow** to the right of legend, then select the desired location.

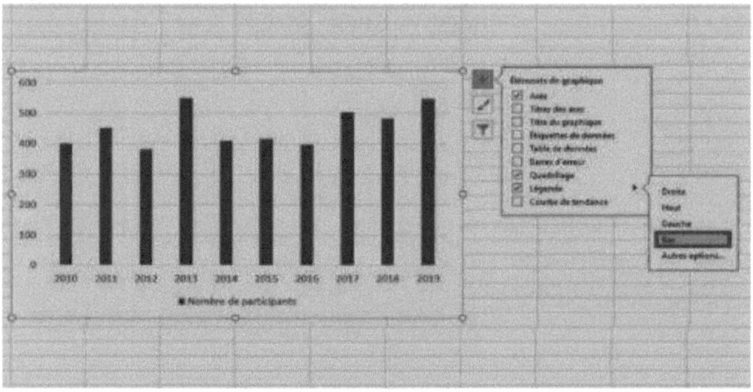

By default, a legend is not allowed to overlap a graphic. But if you're short of space, you can reduce the size of the graphic by clicking on **More options**, then unchecking **the Show legend without overlapping graphic** box.

To delete a caption, **right-click** on it, then click **Delete**.

II.1.6.DATA TABLES AND LABELS

II.1.6.1.DATA TABLE

II.1.6.1.1.DEFINITION

A table of data is **a range of cells in which you can modify the values of certain cells and add new values.**

different answers to a problem.

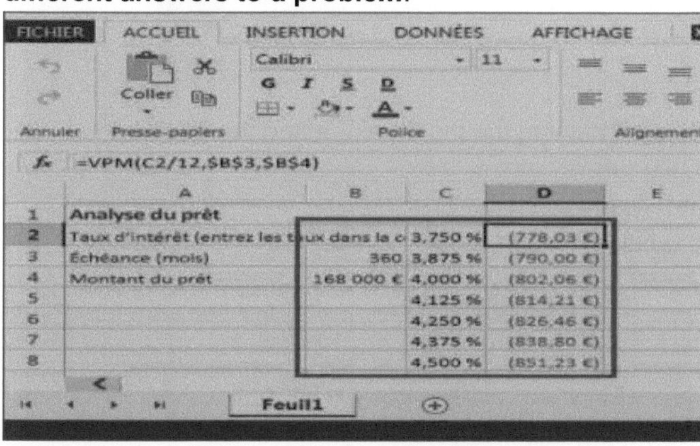

To create a data table, follow these steps:

Don't confuse data tables with Excel spreadsheets.

A data table is a special range that Excel uses to calculate several solutions to a formula.

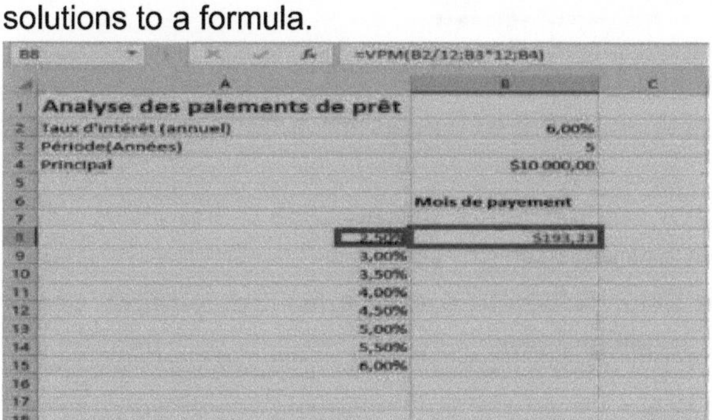

1) Enter the input values:

To type the values in a column, start the column one cell down and one to the left of the cell containing the formula, as shows.   here.

To type the values in a line, start the line one cell up and one to the right of the cell containing the formula.

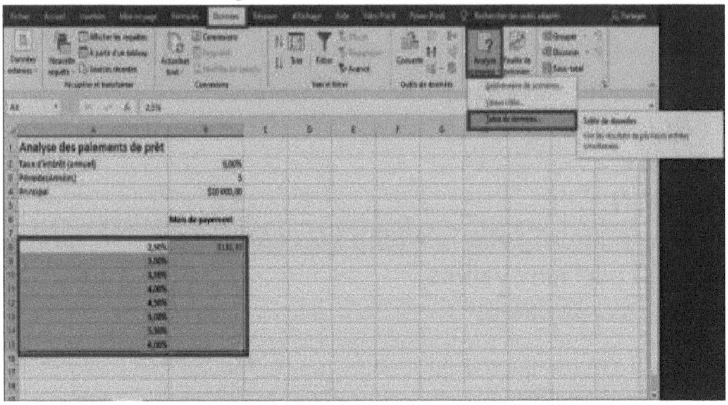

2) Select the range containing the input values and the formula.
3) Click on the Data tab.
4) Click on What-If Analysis.
5) Click on Data table.

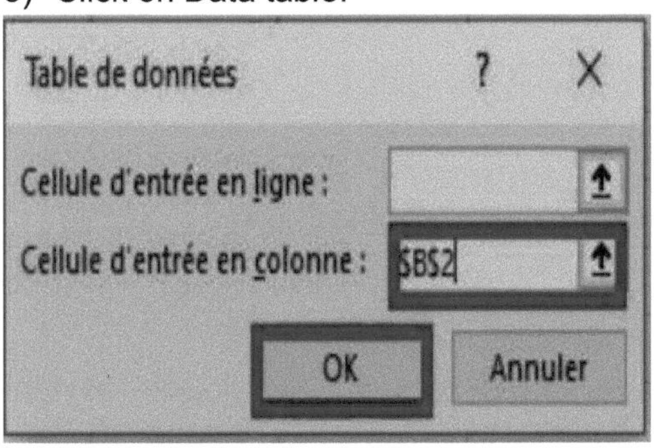

The Data Table dialog box is displayed.

6) Specify the formula cell you want to use as the input cell for the data table:

If the input values are in a column, enter the address of the input cell in the Input cell column text box.

If you have entered the input values in a row, enter the address of the input cell in the Row input cell text box.

7) Click OK.

II.1.6.2.DATA LABEL

To quickly identify a series of data in a graph, you can add data labels to the data points in the graph. By default, the data labels are linked to the values in the worksheet and update automatically when these values are changed.

Data labels make it easier to understand a graph, as they display details about a series of data or individual data points. For example, in the pie chart below, without the data labels, it is difficult to tell that coffee sales represent 38% of total sales. Depending on what you want to highlight in a graph, you can add labels to a series, to all the series (the whole graph) or to a data point.

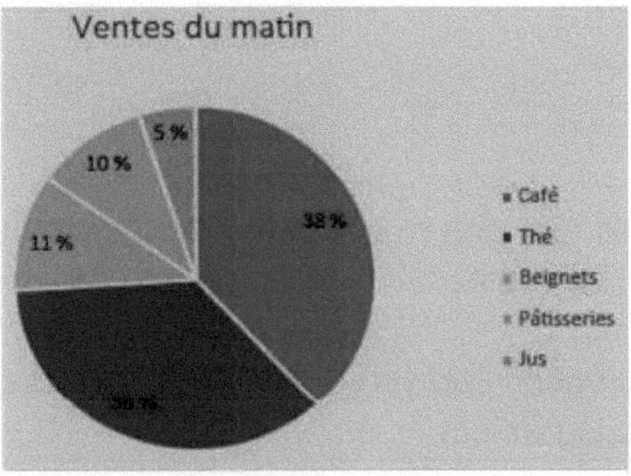

Note: The following procedures apply to Office 2013 and later versions.

II.1.6.2.1.ADDING DATA LABELS TO A GRAPH

1. Click on the data series or graph. To add a label to a data point, after clicking on the series, click on the data point.
2. In the top right-hand corner, next to the graph, click on

Add a chart element + > **data labels**.

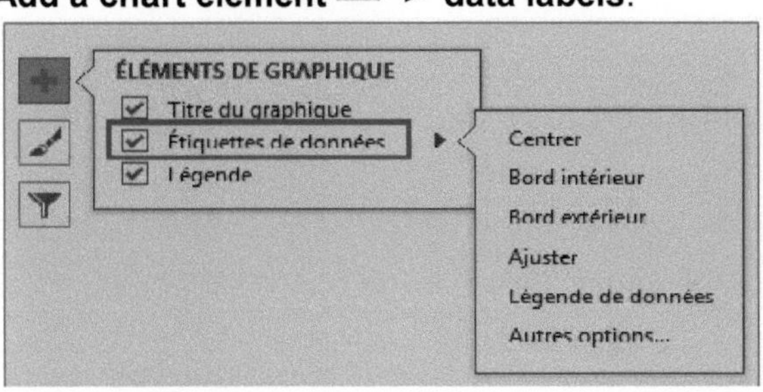

3. To change the location, click on the arrow and choose a location. option.
4. If you want to display the data label in a text bubble, click on **Data caption.**

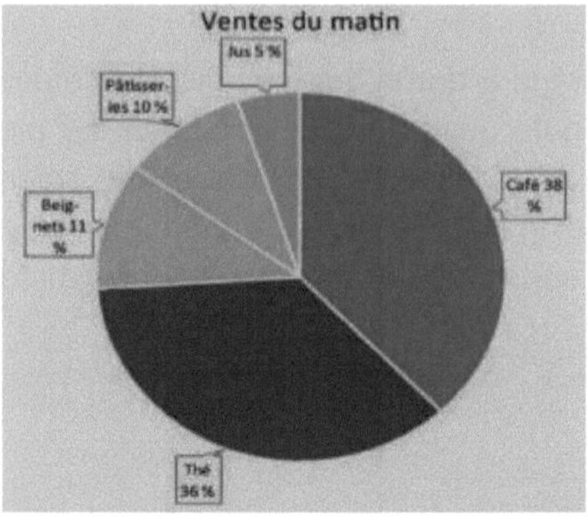

To make it easier to read the labels, you can move them inside the data points or outside the graph. To move a data label, drag it to the desired location.

If you decide that your labels are cluttering up your chart, you can delete them by clicking on them and pressing Delete.

NB: If the text in the data labels is not legible, resize the labels by clicking on them, then enlarging them to the desired size.

II.1.6.2.2.MODIFYING THE APPEARANCE OF DATA LABELS

1. Right-click on the data series or label to display more data, then click **Format data labels**.
2. Click on **Label options** and under **Label content**, choose the options you want.

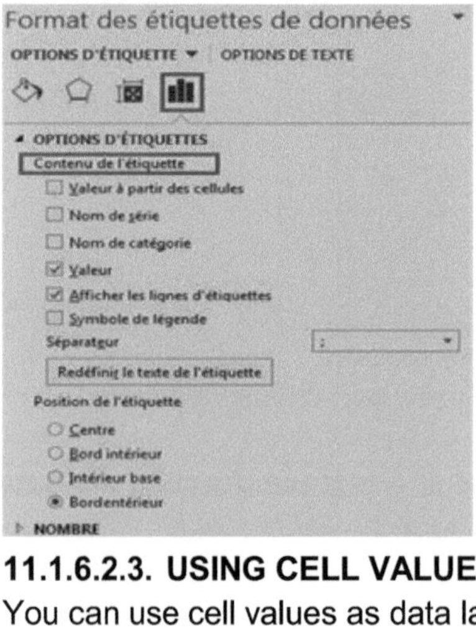

11.1.6.2.3. USING CELL VALUES AS DATA LABELS

You can use cell values as data labels for your graph.

1. Right-click on the data series or label to display more data, then click

on **Format data labels**.

2. Click on **Label options** and, under **Label contains**, tick the **Values from cells** box.

3. When the Data **Label Range** dialog box is displayed, return to the worksheet and select the range for which you want the cell values to be displayed as data labels. In this case, the selected range is displayed in the **Data Label Range** dialog box. Click on **OK**.

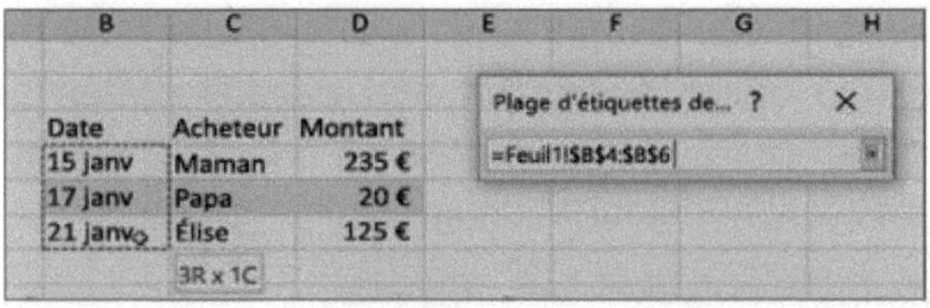

Cell values are now displayed as data labels in your graph.

11.1.6.2.4. CHANGING THE TEXT OF DATA LABELS

1. Click on the data label containing the text to be modified, then click on it again so that it is the only data label selected.
2. Select the existing text, then type the replacement text.
3. Click anywhere outside the data tag.

NB: If you want to add a comment to your graph or if you only have one data label, you can use a text box.

II.1.6.2.5.DELETING DATA LABELS FROM A GRAPH

1. Click on the graph from which you wish to remove data labels. This brings up the **Chart Tools** and the **Design** and **Layout** tabs.
2. Do one of the following:

+ On the **Design** tab, in the **Chart layouts** group, click **Add chart element**, select **Data labels**, then click **None**.

4- Click once on a data tag to select all the data tags in a data set or twice to select a data tag you wish to delete, then press DELETE.

Right-click on a data tag, then click on **Delete**.

Note: This deletes all the data labels in a data set.

3. You can also delete data labels immediately after adding them by clicking on **Undo** EE in the **Quick Access toolbar** or by pressing Ctrl+Z.

11.1.7. BACKGROUND

In Microsoft Excel, you can use an image as a sheet background for display purposes only. A sheet background is not printed and is not stored in an individual worksheet or in an element that you save as a web page.

11.1.7.1. DEFINING THE BACKGROUND FOR THE EXCEL SPREADSHEET

You can add visual interest to a spreadsheet by replacing the background of the standard white sheet with a photo, drawing or other image.

For example, a spreadsheet tracking the amount needed for a future holiday might display a photo of the proposed destination as a background. When choosing the image you want to use as the background, make sure you select an image that doesn't make the spreadsheet text difficult to read. For example, if the text in your spreadsheet is dark, choose a light-coloured image as the background.

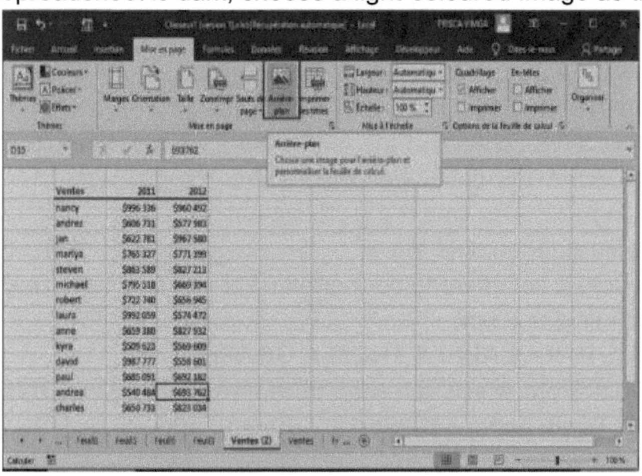

1) Click on the tab of the worksheet you want to customise;
2) Click on the Page Setup tab;
3) Click on Background.

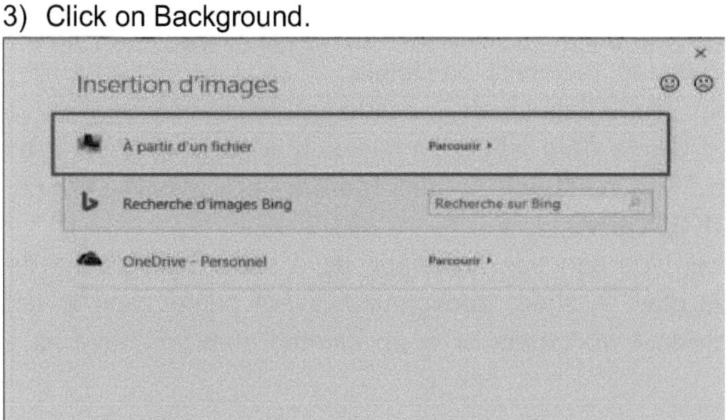

The Insert images dialogue box appears.

4) Click From a file.

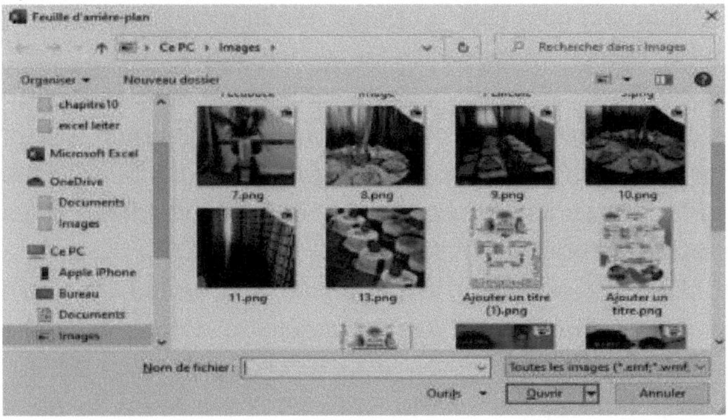

The Sheet background dialogue box appears.

5) Select the location of the image you want to use.

6) Click on the image.

7) Click on Insert.

Excel formats the background of the worksheet with the image you have selected.

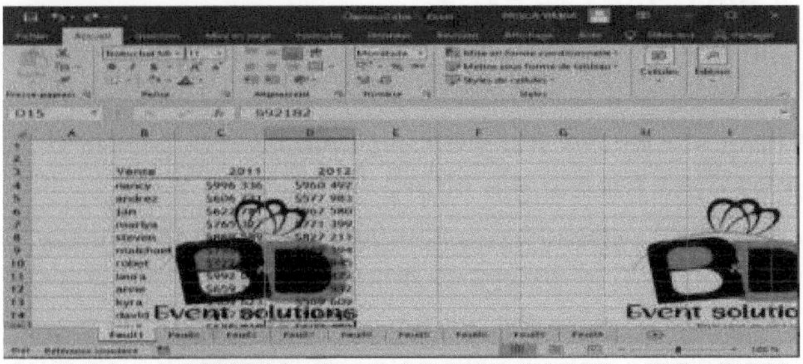

11.1.7.2. APPLY A BACKGROUND COLOUR INSTEAD OF A BACKGROUND IMAGE

Excel does not have a command that changes the background colour of the entire worksheet.

Instead, you must first ;

1) select all the cells in the worksheet by clicking on Select all.

2) Click on the Home tab, on the arrow in the Fill colour drop-down list, then on the colour you want to use.

3) Excel applies the colour to the background of each cell.

II.1.7.3.REMOVING THE BACKGROUND IMAGE FROM THE SPREADSHEET

If you find that having the background image makes it difficult to read the spreadsheet text, you should remove the background.

1) Click on the worksheet tab,

2) click on Page Setup and then click on Delete Background.

Excel deletes the background image from the worksheet.

II.1.8. SECTORS

Pie charts or pie graphs, as they are also known, are a common way of showing how much individual amounts or percentages contribute to the total. In such charts, the whole pie represents 100% of the whole, while the *slices of pie* represent portions of the whole.

People love pie charts, visualisation experts hate them, and the main scientific reason is that the human eye is unable to compare angles accurately.

But if we can't stop making pie charts, why don't we learn to do it properly? A pie chart can be difficult to draw by hand, with the tricky percentages presenting an added challenge.

However, in Microsoft Excel you can create a pie chart in a minute or two. And then, you might want to invest a few extra minutes in customising the charts to give your Excel pie chart a professionally crafted look.

II.1.8.1.CREATING A PIE CHART IN EXCEL

Creating a pie chart in Excel is extremely simple and takes just a few clicks of a button. The key point is to organise the source data correctly in your spreadsheet and choose the most appropriate type of pie chart.

1) Prepare the source data for the pie chart.

Unlike other graphs, pie charts require the source data to be organised in a column or row. In fact, only one series of data can be plotted in a pie chart.

You can also include a column or row with category names, which must be the first column or row in the selection. The category names will appear in the pie chart legend and/or data labels.

In general, here are some of the characteristics of a pie chart:

- Only one set of data is plotted in the graph.
- All data values are greater than zero.
- There are no empty rows or columns.
- There should be no more than 7 to 9 categories of data, as too many sectors can clutter up your graph and make it difficult to understand.

We are going to create a pie chart using the following data:

	A	B	C
1	Fruits	Pourcentages	
2	Ananas	36%	
3	Orange	14%	
4	Citron	13%	
5	Raison	28%	
6	Pomme	9%	
7			

2) Insert a pie chart in the current worksheet.

Once you have organised your source data correctly, select it, go to the *Insert* tab and choose the type of chart you want. In this example, we create the most common 2D pie chart:

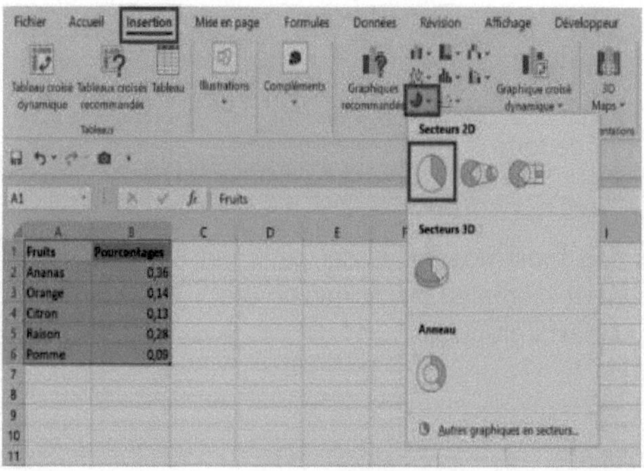

Include column or row headings in the selection if you want the column/value row heading to appear automatically in the title of your pie chart.

3) Choose the pie chart style (optional).

Once the new pie chart is inserted into your worksheet, you can go to the *Chart Creation* tab / *Charts* group and try out different pie chart styles to choose the one that best suits your data.

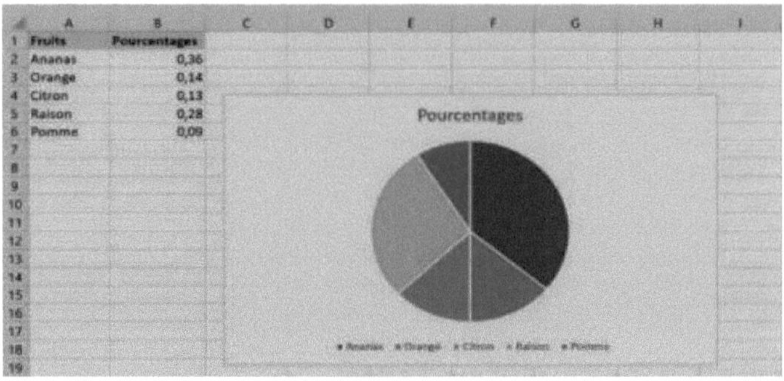

11.1.8.2. CREATING DIFFERENT TYPES OF PIE CHARTS IN EXCEL

When you create a pie chart in Excel, you can choose one of the following subtypes:

- 2D pie chart
- 3D pie chart
- Tarte a tarte or Barre de tarte
- Ring graph

2D Excel pie charts

This is the standard and most popular Excel pie chart that you would probably use most often. It is created by clicking on the 2D pie chart icon in the *Insert* tab / **Charts** group.

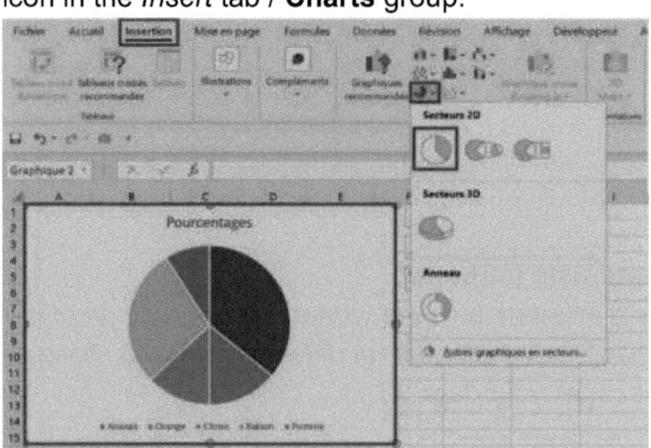

3D Excel pie charts

A 3D pie chart is similar to a 2D pie chart, but it displays the data on a third *axis.*

depth (perspective).

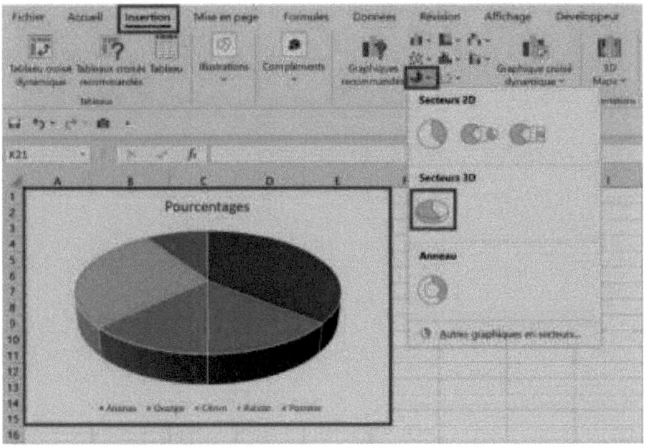

When you create 3D pie charts in Excel, you have access to additional features such as 3D rotation and perspective.

Bar and pie charts

If your Excel pie chart has too many small slices, you may want to create a pie chart and display small slices on an additional pie, which is a slice of the main pie.

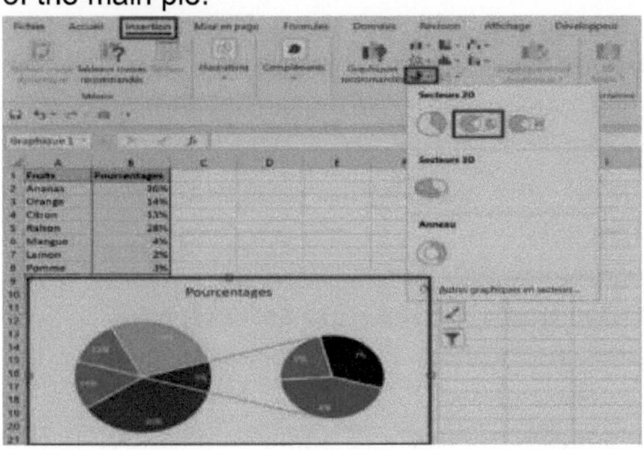

The sector bar chart is very similar to the sector chart, except that the selected slices are displayed on a secondary bar chart.

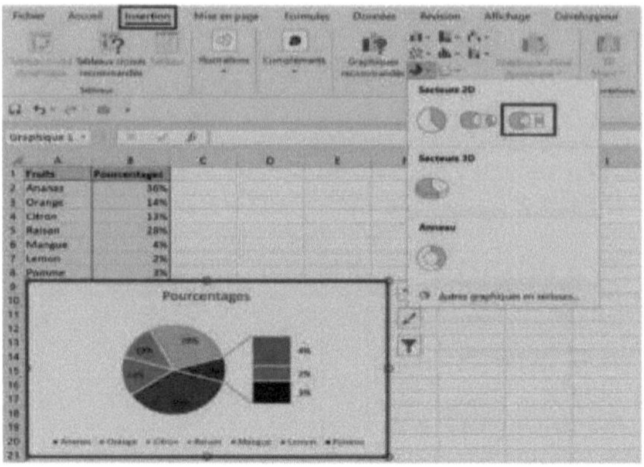

When you create a bar chart of sectors in Excel, the last 3 categories of data are moved to the second chart by default (even if they are the largest categories!). And because the default choice doesn't always work well, you can either :

. Sort the source data in your spreadsheet in descending order so that the worst-performing elements are included in the secondary graph, or

- Select the data categories to be moved to the second graph.

Choice of data categories for the secondary graph

To manually select the data categories to be moved to the secondary graph, proceed as follows:

1. Right-click on any slice of your pie chart and select *Format data series...* from the context menu.
2. In the *Layout data series* pane, under *Series options*, select one of the following options from the drop-down list **Separate series from**:

- *Position* - lets you select the number of categories to move to the second graph.
- *Value*- allows you to specify a threshold (minimum value) below which the data categories are moved to the additional graph.
- *Percentage value* - this is like the value, but here you specify the percentage threshold.
- *Custom* - allows you to manually select any slice of the pie chart in your spreadsheet, then specify whether you want to place it in the main or secondary chart.

In most cases, defining the percentage threshold is the most reasonable choice, but it all depends on your source data and personal preferences. The following screenshot illustrates the splitting of the data set by *percentage value*:

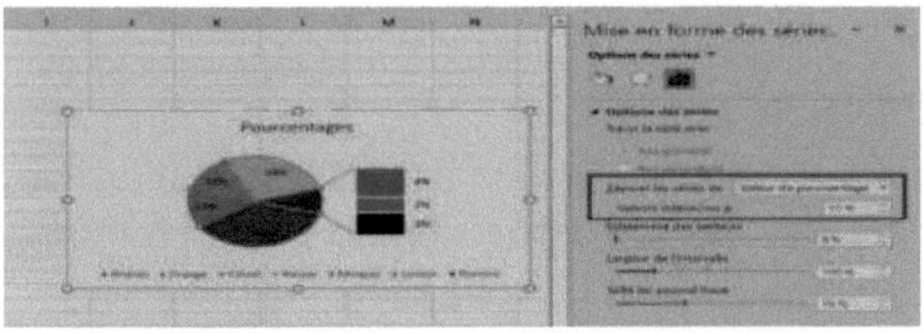
Pourcentages
Mise en forme des séries

CHAPTER III

SIMPLE CALCULATIONS IN EXCEL

To perform basic mathematical operations, such as addition, subtraction, multiplication or division, as well as combining numbers and producing numerical results, use the following arithmetic operators:

Arithmetic operator	Meaning	Example
+ (plus sign)	Addition	= 3 + 3
	Subtraction	=3-3
- (minus sign)	Negation	= -3
* (asterisk)	Multiplication	= 3 * 3
/ (slash)	Division	= 3/3

111.1. ADDITION

You can use a simple formula to add up the numbers in a range (a group of cells), but the SUM function is easier to use when working with several numbers. For example, =SUM(A2:A6) is less likely to have input errors than =A2+A3+A4+A5+A6.

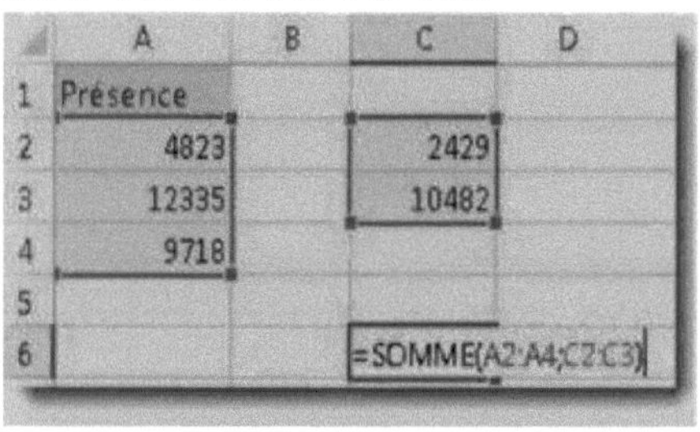

Here's a formula that uses two cell ranges: **=SUMM(A2:A4;C2:C3) sums** the numbers in ranges A2:A4 and C2:C3. Press Enter to obtain the total 39787.

To create the formula :

1) Type **=SOMM** in a cell, followed by an opening parenthesis **(** ;

2) To enter the first range of formulas, called the *argument* (the data the formula needs to run), type **A2:A4** (or select cell A2 and drag to cell A6);

3) To perform this task, **use the arithmetic operator * (asterisk)**. For example, if you type =5*10 in a cell, the cell will display the result 50. Next;

4) Type the second argument, **C2:C3** (or drag to select cells).

5) Type a closing parenthesis), then press Enter.

III.2.SUBTRACTION

a) Type a number in cells C1 and D1. For example, 5 and 3.

b) In cell E1, type an equals sign (=) **to** start creating the **formula**.

c) After the equals sign, type C1-D1.

d) **Press** RETURN. If you use the numbers **in** this example, the result is 2.

111.3. MULTIPLICATION

To perform this task, **use the arithmetic operator * (asterisk)**. For example, if you type =5*10 in a cell, the cell will display the result 50.

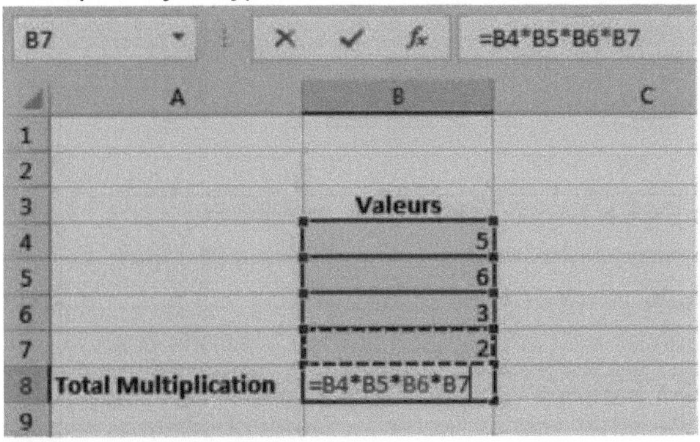

111.4. PERCENTAGE

When calculating percentages in Excel, you save yourself steps like multiplying by 100, as the program takes care of the formatting itself as soon as you apply the % style (more on this below). The formula for calculating percentages in Excel is :

Number/Total number=Percentage

Let's look at a concrete example of a percentage calculation: To manage his inventory, a retailer uses a spreadsheet that lists the products bought and sold. The number of products bought by the shopkeeper appears in column B and the number of products sold in column C. To calculate the corresponding percentages in column D, enter the following formula (and press [Enter]): =C2/B2

D2 f_x =C2/B2

	A	B	C	D
1	Produit	Achats	Ventes	Pourcentage ventes
2	Chemises	40	29	73%
3	Jupes	50	32	64%
4	Chemisiers	30	23	77%
5	Pantalons	35	25	71%
6	T-shirts	50	41	82%
7	Pullovers	40	34	85%
8	Chapeaux	20	12	60%
9	Sacs	30	19	63%
10	Chaussures	25	23	92%
11				

111.5. SIMPLE PERCENTAGE FORMULA IN EXCEL

Double-click on the bottom right-hand corner of the cell (here D2) to easily transfer the formula to the following rows. Excel will automatically apply the formula as soon as you enter other data in columns B and C.

111.6. APPLY THE PERCENTAGE STYLE IN EXCEL

The result may not yet be what you expected: instead of percent values, you see decimal values in your Excel table.

D2 f_x =C2/B2

	A	B	C	D
1	Produit	Achats	Ventes	Pourcentage ventes
2	Chemises	40	29	0,725
3	Jupes	50	32	0,64
4	Chemisiers	30	23	0,766666667
5	Pantalons	35	25	0,714285714
6	T-shirts	50	41	0,82
7	Pullovers	40	34	0,85
8	Chapeaux	20	12	0,6
9	Sacs	30	19	0,633333333
10	Chaussures	25	23	0,92
11				

This is what your Excel table looks like without the % formatting.

For Excel to add the % sign and round the result by automatically applying the percentage style, you first need to set it up: the quick selection of the cell format for setting up percentages in Excel can be found in the "Home" tab, in the "Number" option group (between "Alignment" and "Styles").

Simply click on the % sign to select the percentage style. You can do this for a single cell, a range of cells, an entire column or an entire row. In this example, we have calculated the percentages in column D by having first select the corresponding cells :

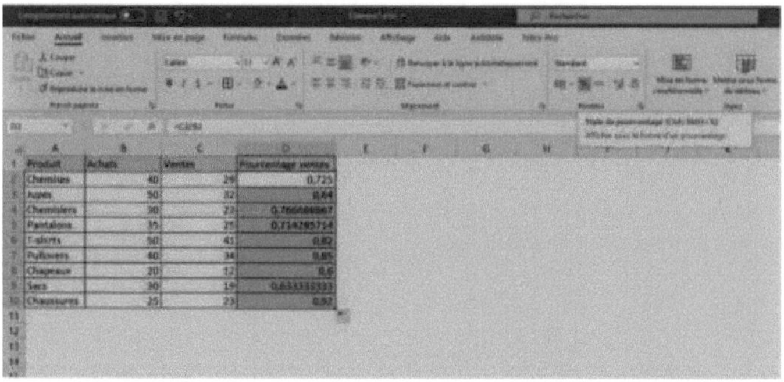

Click on the % sign to apply the percentage style to your Excel cells. Alternatively, you can apply the percentage style using the shortcut [Ctrl] + [Shift] + [%] (as shown in the screenshot).

111.7. CUSTOMISE THE PERCENTAGE STYLE IN EXCEL

If you proceed as described above, the percentages should be displayed without decimals, in line with the default settings. Don't worry, you can customise the style very easily by clicking on the little arrow at the bottom right of the 'Number' options group. Alternatively, you can right-click on the cell you want after selecting it, then select 'Cell Format' from the menu that opens.

To modify percentages in Excel, you can now define which decimal places should appear. For example, if you want to display two digits after the decimal point, choose "2".

Then click on "OK".

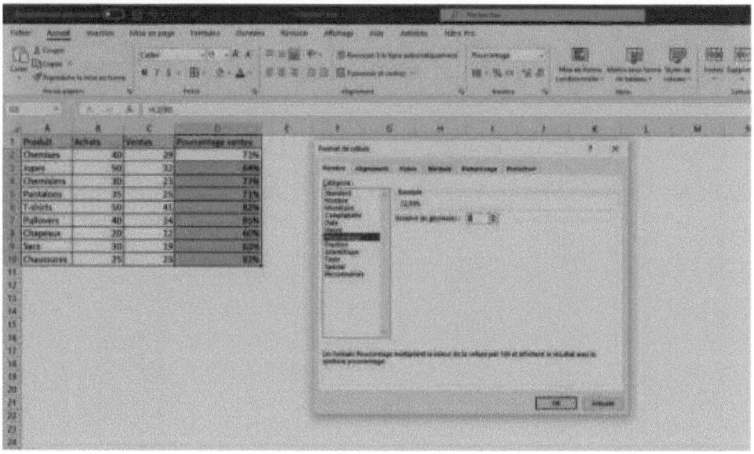

Enter the number of decimal places to display for percentages in Excel.

In the same window, in the "Custom" category, you can also display percentages, either without decimal places or with two decimal places.

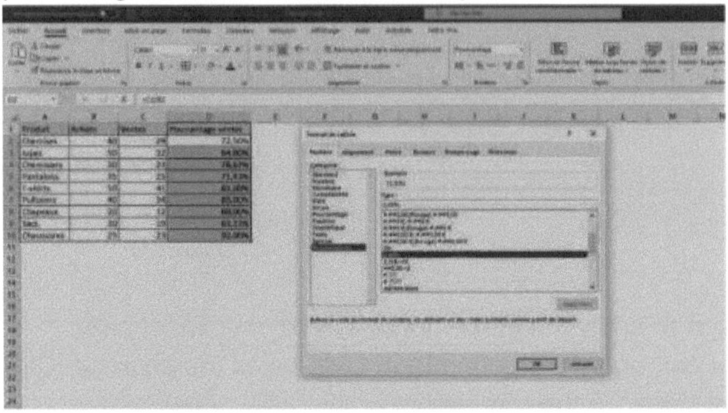

You can display percentages with or without decimals by going to Customise.

CHAPTER IV

EXCEL FUNCTIONS

111.8. ONCTION SOMME

The Excel function **SUM** calculates the sum of a series of values. Usage :=SUM(values)

EXAMPLE

The SUM function has its own shortcut, so you don't need to search for SUM in the list of functions.

Click on the cell containing the sum and then on the "Somme automatique" () :

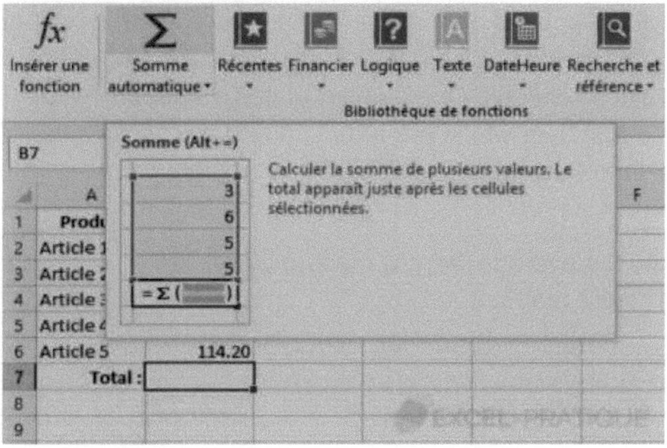

A list of values is preselected automatically.

If it is correct, press Enter, if not, make another selection and press Enter.

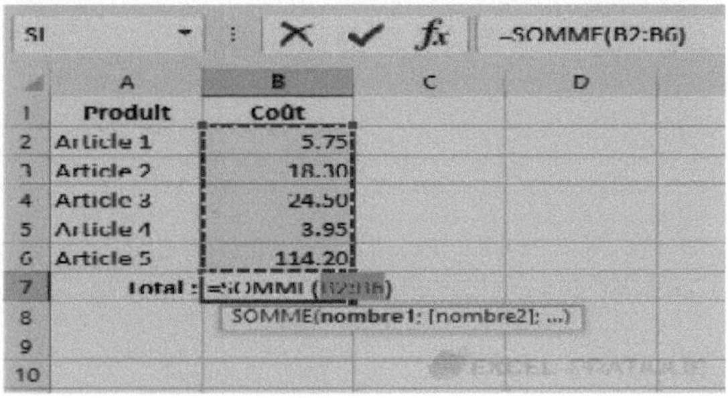

The sum is calculated :

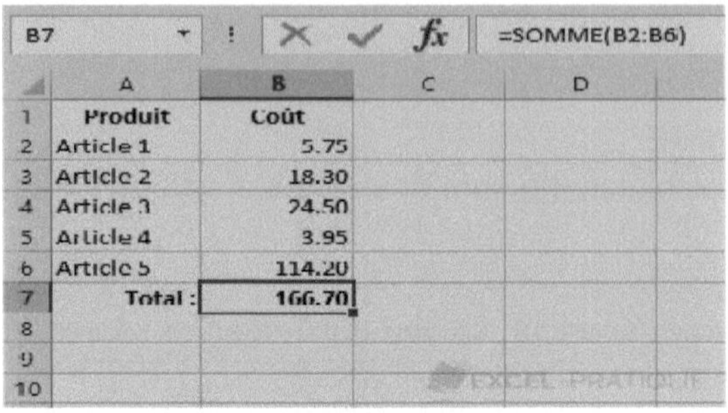

B7 | =SOMME(B2:B6)

	A	B	C	D
1	Produit	Coût		
2	Article 1	5.75		
3	Article 2	18.30		
4	Article 3	24.50		
5	Article 4	3.95		
6	Article 5	114.20		
7	Total :	166.70		
8				
9				
10				

IV.2. AVERAGE FUNCTION

The average function is used to calculate the average of a set of numerical values. The average of a set of numerical values is equal to the sum of these values divided by the number of these values.

Suppose we have 5 numbers which are a, b, c, d and e. The average of these numbers will therefore be:

$$\frac{a+b+c+d+e}{5}$$

In Excel, to calculate the average, here is the formula:

=MOYENNE(cell1 ;cell2 ;cell3...)

EXAMPLE

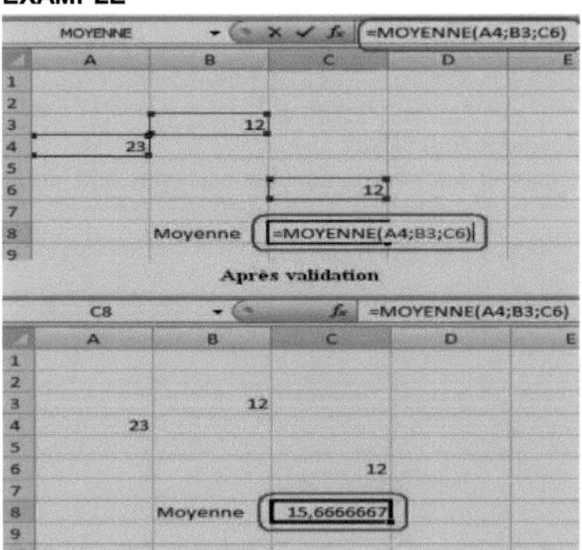

If the cells containing the numbers we are working on are aligned, the formula is

=MOYENNE (cell1:cell n). For example, if the numbers are in cells A1, A2, A3, A4 and A5, the average can be calculated as follows: **=MOYENNE(A1:A5)**.

If the numbers are in cell A1, B1, C1, D1 and E1, the Average can be calculated:

=MEAN(A1:E1).

CHAPTER V

USING OUTLOOK

V.1.DISCOVERING OUTLOOK

Outlook is an e-mail client and organiser from Microsoft and part of the Microsoft Office suite. It is primarily used as an e-mail client, but also includes functions such as a calendar, contact manager, task manager note-taking, diary and Web browsing.[1]

V.2.DISCOVERING THE CALENDAR

The calendar is the Outlook planning component, fully integrated with email, contacts and other functions.

The Calendar lets you create appointments and events, organise meetings, display group schedules and more.[2]

V.3.CREATING A CALENDAR

To create a calendar with Outlook, follow these steps :

1. In **Outlook**.com, select Calendar. > Add a calendar > **Create a calendar**.
2. Give your calendar a name.
3. Personalise your calendar with a colour, a charm or both.
4. Optional: add your calendar to an existing calendar group.
5. Select Save.

V.4. CREATING AN APPOINTMENT

To create an appointment,

1. click on the **date and time of** the appointment
2. click on the **New appointment** icon

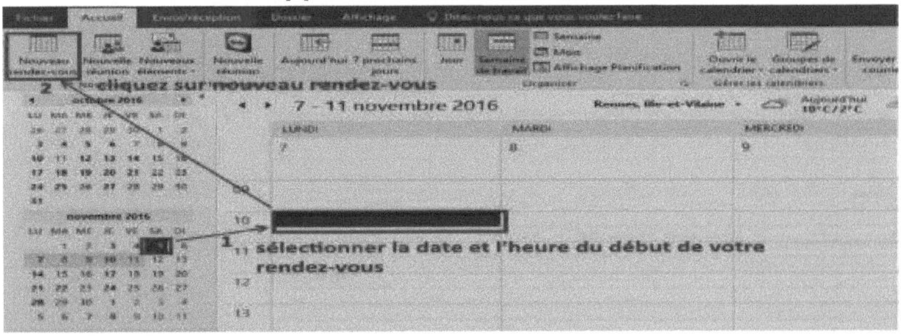

3. then fill in the fields on the form, specifying :

a. **the purpose of** the meeting

[1] https://mspoweruser.com, consulted on 03/10/2023 at 4h9'.

[2] https://support.microsoft.com, consulted on 03/10/2023 at 4h20'.

b. **^'location**
c. **start and end date and time**
d. **type of display** on your calendar: *busy, away...* (visible to all those with whom you share your calendar - *busy* means you don't want to be disturbed during this appointment)
e. **appointment reminder**: this means that you will receive a reminder message here *15 minutes before the scheduled time*
f. **classify by colour category** (red, blue, ...) *optional field*

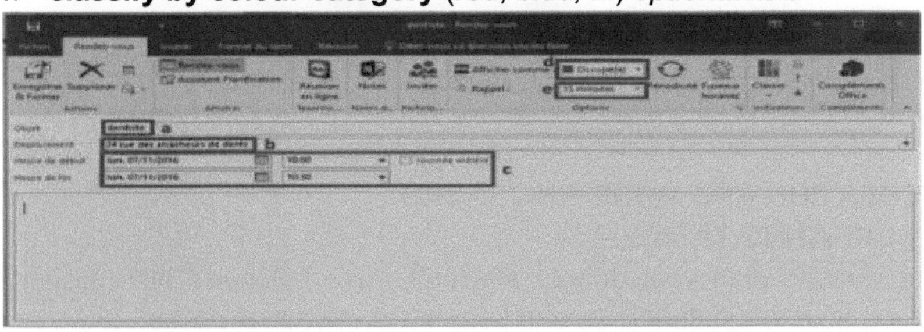

Finally, complete the creation by clicking on the **Save & Close** icon.
Outlook lets you **change your appointment** directly with **the mouse**:

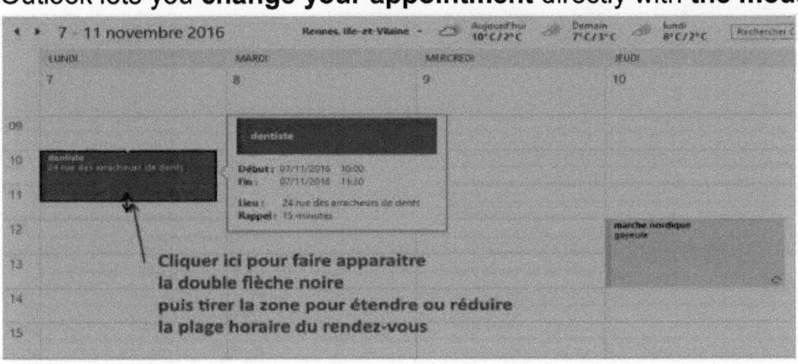

Outlook lets you **move your appointment** directly **with the mouse**:

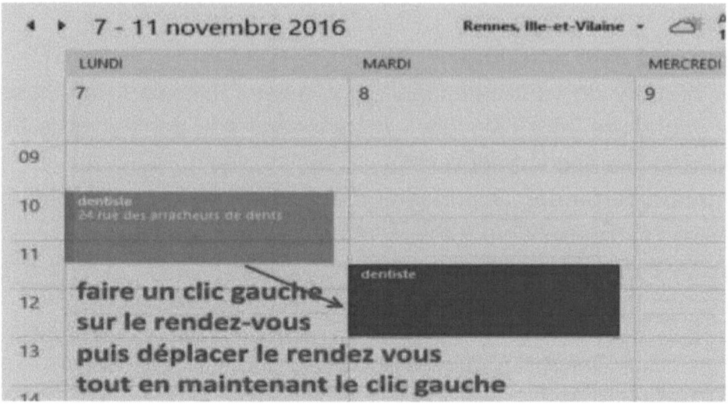

V.5.CREATING AND MODIFYING TASKS

V.5.1.CREATING TASKS

If you want to plan your activity efficiently, use Outlook's task system. You'll be able to set deadlines and keep track of your activities.

IIn **Outlook 2013 and 2010**, click on *New items*, then *Task*.

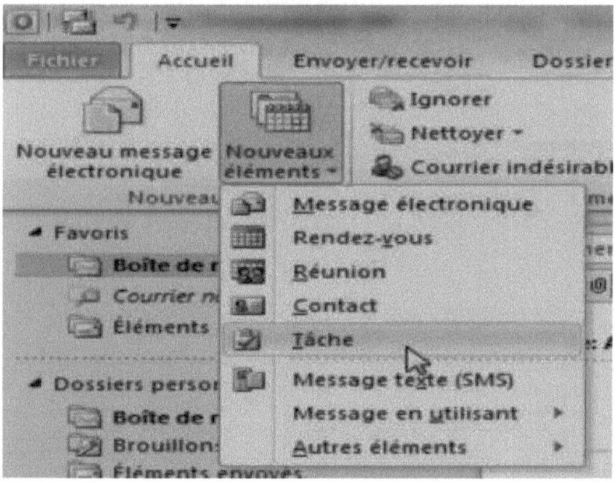

©In **other versions**, click on the small arrow to the right of the *New* button on the toolbar, then select *Spot*.

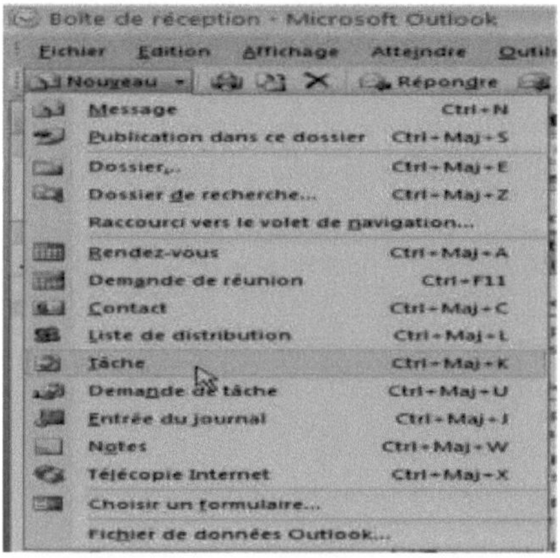

In the window that opens, type the name of the task in the *Subject* field, then specify the start date (if required) and the due date.

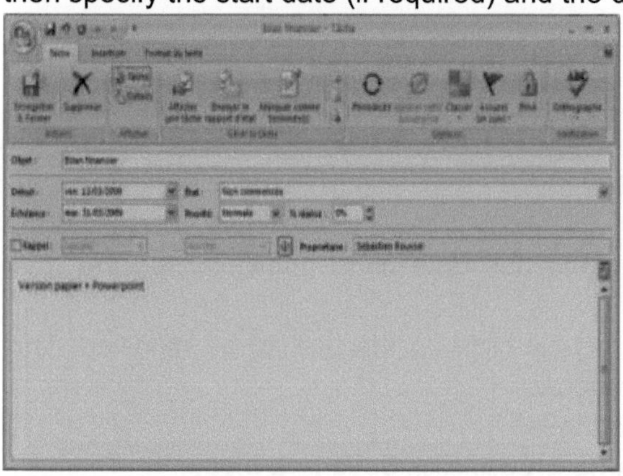

You can also specify the status of the task (*Not started, In progress, Completed, Waiting for someone else* or *Deferred),* the priority (*Low, Normal* or *High)* and finally the percentage completed.
You can also type the details in the box at the bottom of the window.
Options:
. In the latest versions of Outlook, you can **classify your task** by clicking on the *Classify* button (in Outlok 2007) or *Categories* (in other versions).
• By ticking the *Reminder* box, you can ask Outlook to **remind you of the task** on a date in the future of your choice .
. To **assign the task to someone else**, click on the *Assign a task* button (or *Assign a task*) and select the relevant contacts in the *a* field.
• By clicking on the *Details* button or tab, you can **enter details** of the

work carried out, such as working time, mileage or invoicing information. Finally, click on the *Save and Close* button to finish.

To manage stains

To display the list of tasks, display the Outlook *Tasks* module: click on the appropriate icon in the navigation pane.

Simply tick a task to indicate that it has been completed.

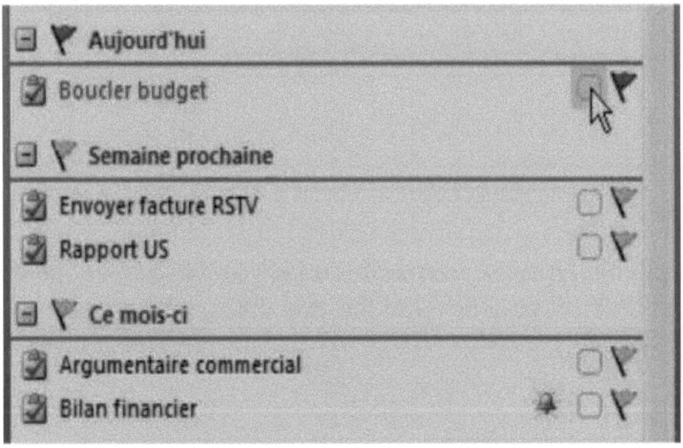

V.5.2.MODIFYING A TASK

It is sometimes necessary to modify a task, for example, to change the percentage of completion, the due date or to add notes on the work done.

1. In the task list pane, double-click on the task to be modified. This action will open the task window.
2. Make the necessary changes.
3. In the **Home** tab, **Actions group**, click **Save and close.**

V.6.ASSIGNMENT OF TASKS

Tasks help you keep track of your tasks. You can also assign tasks to other people.

1. In the navigation bar, click on **Tasks**, then on **New task**, or open an existing task.
2. Click **on Assign a task.**

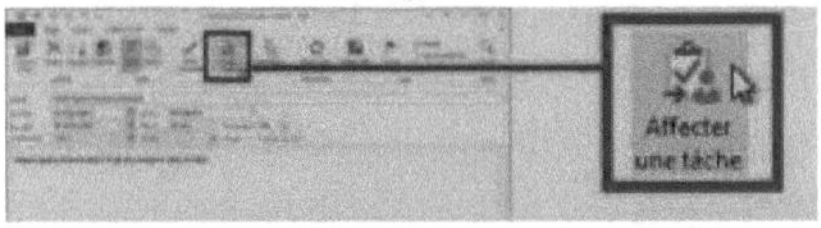

3. In the **To** field, enter a name or an e-mail address.
4. Enter **the subject,** start date and **expiry** date.

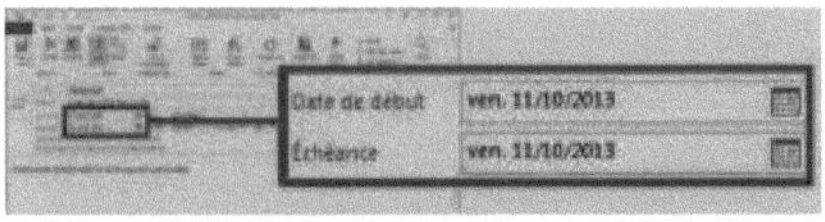

5. If you want the task to recur, click **Recurrence**, select the options you want, then click **OK.**
6. Click on **Send**.

Note: If you assign a periodic task, a copy of that task remains in your task list but is never updated. If you check the **Send status report** when completed box, you will receive status reports for each completed instance of the task.

V.7.PLANNING OF PERIODIC MEETINGS

Invite participants to a meeting with Outlook. You'll be sure to reach everyone without wasting time talking to voicemail!

The participant replies and the meeting is automatically added to their calendar. If they delete it, you will be informed.

If you change any information, for example the location of the meeting, Outlook will remember your list of participants, and everyone will have the information. You'll be sure not to forget anyone.

Do you need to hold your meetings on Tuesdays for the next 3 weeks? Use the periodicity.

If you want to be as efficient as possible, create a distribution list for each committee and use it when you call your meeting.

V.7.1.PROCEDURE FOR SENDING A MEETING REQUEST

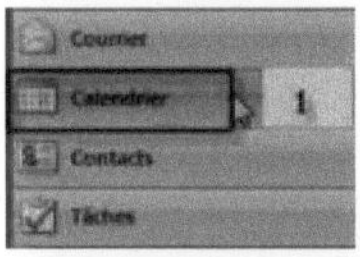

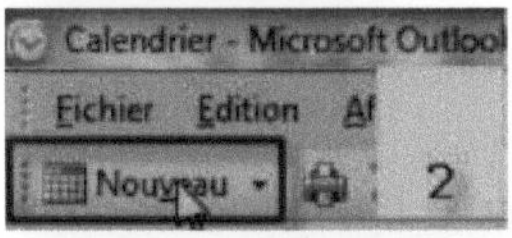

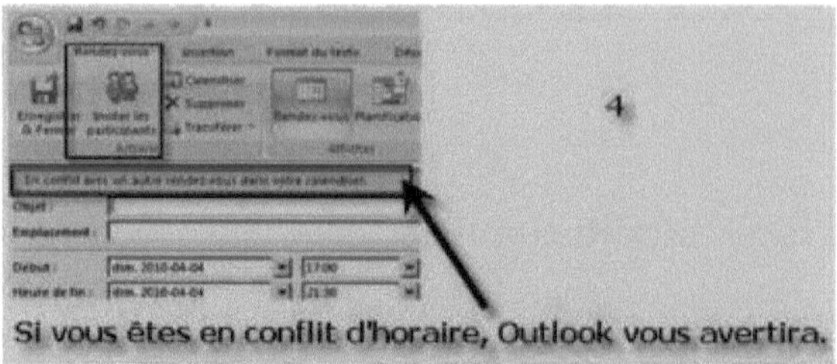

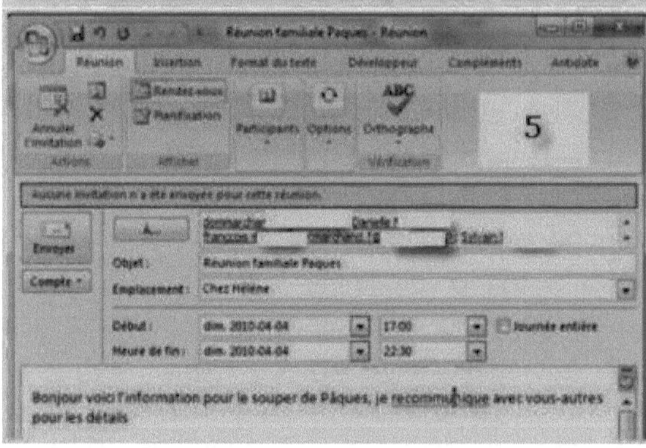

Fill in the information. For **the A**: create and use a distribution list.

Check answers:

. Request an answer ;

. Allow new timetable proposals. If you have a group with several participants, avoid ticking this option.

Meeting follow-up for the organiser

Example of a participant's response

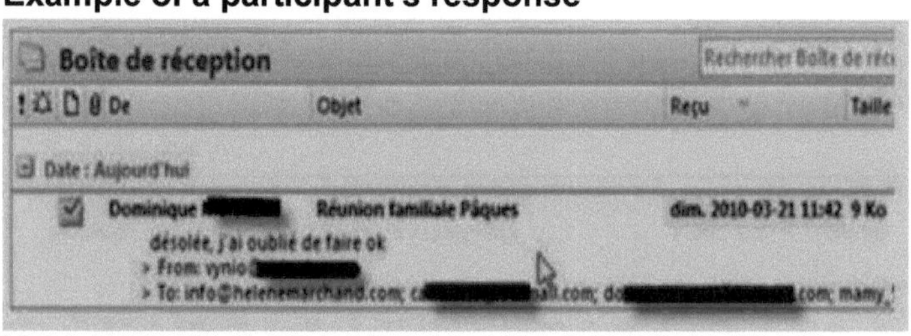

V.7.2.EXAMPLE OF PARTICIPANT CONFIRMATION

Click on the **schedule** icon to add or remove participants. Use a tick to specify the participants who will receive the information when the changes are made.

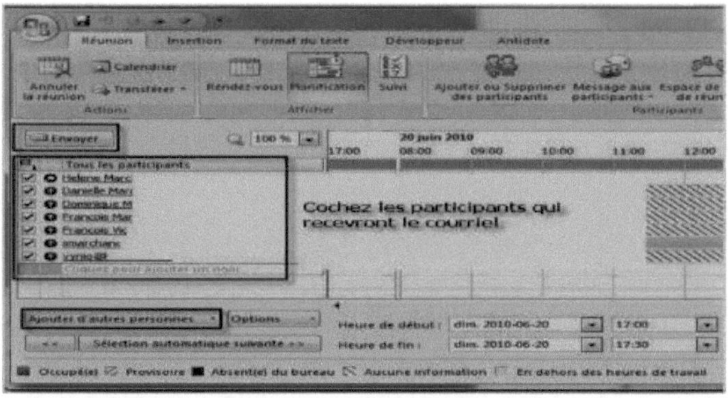

Click on the **schedule** icon to add or remove participants. Use a tick to specify the participants who will receive the information when the changes are made.

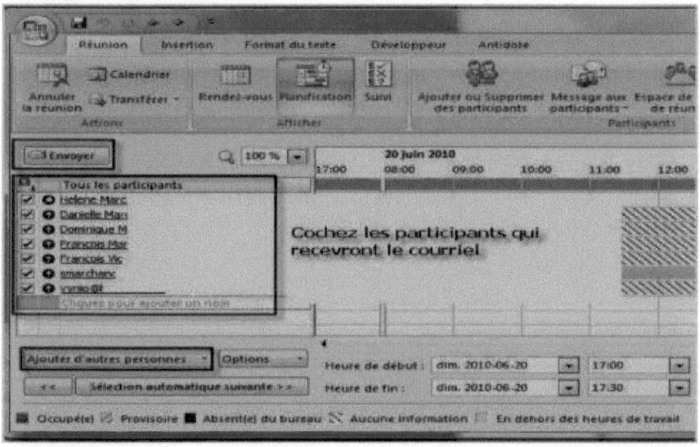

V.7.3.MAKING CHANGES TO A MEETING AND SENDING AN UPDATE

Organisers can modify their meeting request by double-clicking on the appointment. They can then make corrections and send an update using the appropriate button. Outlook will ask you to confirm who you want to send your update to.

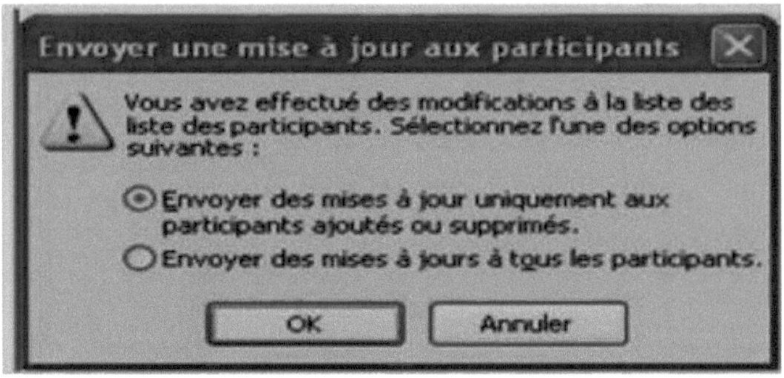

NB: The person who sends the first email requesting a meeting is the organiser. Once you are the meeting organiser, you remain the meeting organiser.

A participant who declines a meeting remains on the list of participants.

CHAPTER VI

WORD DOCUMENT PROCESSING

EXERCISES

CHAPTER VII

USING THE PRINTER

VII.1.INSTALLING THE PRINTER

1) **Read** your printer's **instructions carefully.** No two printers are alike and there are many different models. So, before reading what follows, consult the installation manual supplied by the manufacturer. On the manufacturer's website, you'll probably find a link to download the specific manual for your printer in PDF format.

2) **Connect the printer to the computer.** Please note: you must connect the printer to a USB port on the computer, not to a USB port on a router.

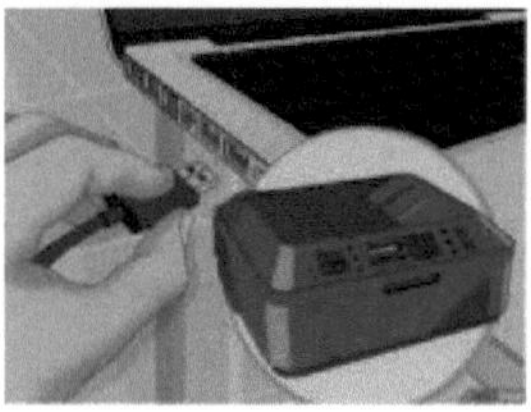

o Don't forget not of course, to connect your printer to a socket
electric!

3) **Switch on the printer.** You should hear a small
noise when switched on, and see indicator lights come on.

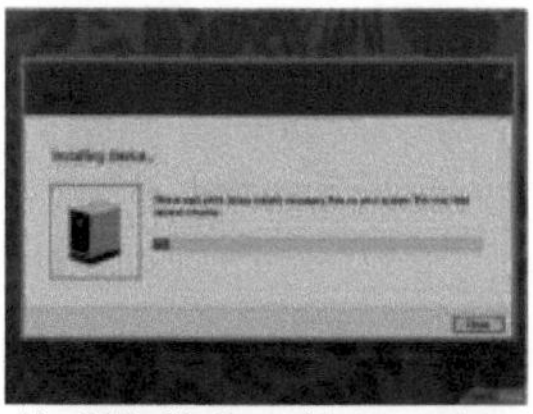

4) **Wait for it to start up.** The operating system detects as soon as a printer is connected. Nowadays, recent versions of Windows and OS X have the latest drivers installed from the outset. If this is not the case, the system will go and look for the drivers, which requires you to have an Internet connection. Things have come a long way in recent years. But not everyone has the latest computer, the latest printer or the latest version of Windows or OS X. If that's the case for you, the following should be of interest.

5) **Install the software sold with the printer.** The CD-ROM supplied with the printer contains everything you need to make it work properly. There are even programmes that allow you to take advantage of some of the printer's specific features. If the printer is not automatically recognised by the operating system and you no longer have the installation cederom, go straight on to the next step.

o If you see that your printer configures itself, you don't need to do anything special, other than wait for the settings to finish. You don't need to add anything.

6) **Download the drivers from the manufacturer's website.** If you do not have an installation cederom, or if the printer does not install automatically, go to the manufacturer's website to obtain the appropriate drivers. You will need the exact part number of your printer: it is printed

on one side of your machine.

NB: To find the drivers for your printer, go to your favourite search engine (Google, for example), and type in a query like "printer drivers *manufacturer model*".

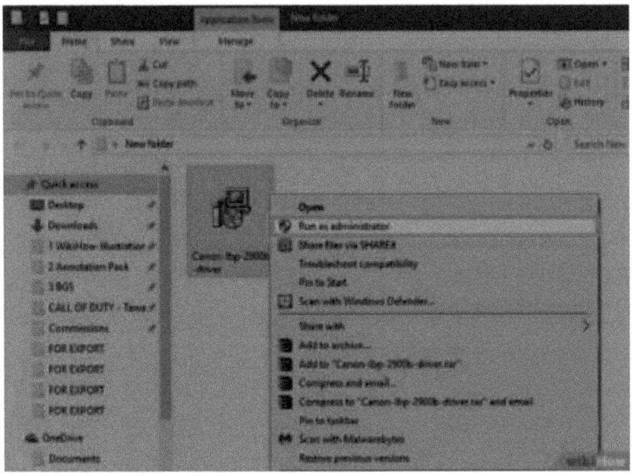

7) **Install the drivers.** After downloading and restarting your computer, you should be able to print from any software that handles document printing.

VII.2.USING THE PRINTER

1) Using a printer, even a basic printer, is extremely easy to do. There are many printer models to choose from. You have the basis for your all-in-one printer. The all-in-one printer works pretty much like the regular printer, you just have a lot more buttons to push.

2) Make sure that your printer is connected correctly before using it.

3) Open the page you want to print. If you are on the Internet and want to print something from there. All you have to do is go up to drop, then down to the page set up. This will give you more printing options to choose from. When you have finished setting up the page you can check if you have the right printer branch by clicking on "Printer" at the bottom. Once everything looks good, click "OK" and now your page should print.

4) Open a . Doc" file if that's where your page is that you need to print . When you are ready to print go to "File" and "Print Setup". Again you can choose how you would like your page to look and check and make sure the correct printer is set up. If your page is set up the way you want it, simply click on the printer icon in the toolbar or go to 'File' and then 'Print'.

5) Using a printer much more time will start to wear down your ink

supply. Some printer models let you know when your ink cartridge is low. If you have a larger printer you'll just have to go by what the printed page looks like. If it's very worn and faded, then it's time to install a new ink cartridge.

CHAPTER VIII

DATA REPRESENTATION

V III.1.DIGITAL INFORMATION

Digital information is **information that has been quantified and sampled**, as opposed to "analogue" information, which is "raw" information that has not been quantified or sampled[3] .

V III.2.NUMBERING SYSTEMS

V III.2.1.DECIMAL SYSTEM

This is the numbering system used in everyday life. In this system, any number N is expressed using ten digits: 0, 1, 2, ..., 9. The number base is then said to be B=10.

Example:

The number 1356.724 corresponds to :

$$1356{,}724=1000+300+50+6+0.7+0.02+0.004$$

$$1356{,}724=10^3+3*10^2+5*10^1+6*10^0+7*10^{-1}+2*10^{-2}+4*10^{-3}$$

Alors: $(1356{,}724)_{10}=1*B^3+3*B^2+5*B^1+6*B^0+7*B^{-1}+2*B^{-2}+4*B^{-3}$

avec B=10.

V III.2.2.BINARY SYSTEM

In this numbering system, all numbers are expressed using the digits 0 and 1, these two digits are called bits (contraction of nary digi).BIT

For the Binary system, the number base is B=2. The coefficients

$a_i : 0.\ B\text{-}1 \rightarrow 0{,}1$

This basis is very useful in digital electronics for distinguishing between two logic states. We write :

$$(a_n a_{n-1} \dots a_0)_2 = a_n 2^n + a_{n-1} 2^{n-1} + \dots + a_1 2^1 + a_0 2^0$$

The right-hand side of the equation gives the decimal value of the binary number written on the left.

- a_0 : Le bit le plus à droite est le bit de poids le plus faible ou bien le moins significatif (*LSB : Low Significant Bit*).
- a_n : Le bit le plus à gauche est le bit de poids le plus fort ou bien le plus significatif (*MSB : Most Significant Bit*)

Example

$$(1011{,}01)_2=1*2^3+0*2^2+1*2^1+1*2^0+0*2^{-1}+1*2^{-2}$$

The transition from the binary system to the decimal system is called decoding, and the transition from the decimal system to the binary system is called coding:

Moving from system X to system Y is called **Transcoding**.

---

[3] https://www.techno-science.net, consulted on 04/10/2023 at 09:53 am

VIII.2.3.BINARY TO DECIMAL CONVERSION

To convert a binary number into a decimal, simply use the relationship (2), where B=2 :

$$(N)_{10}=a_n B^n + a_{n-1} B^{n-1} + \dots + a_1 B^1 + a_0 + a_{-1} B^{-1} + \dots a_{-m} B^{-m}$$

$$(N)_{10}=a_n 2^n + a_{n-1} 2^{n-1} + \dots + a_1 2^1 + a_0 + a_{-1} 2^{-1} + \dots a_{-m} 2^{-m}$$

Example:

a) Convert the binary number $(11010)_2$ to decimal

$$(11010)_2 = 1*2^4+1*2^3+0*2^2+1*2^1+0*2^0$$

$$(11010)_2 = 16+8+2$$

$$(11010)_2 = (26)_{10}$$

$$(110001{,}001)_2 = 1*2^5+1*2^4+0*2^3+0*2^2+0*2^1+1*2^0+0*2^{-1}+0*2^{-2}+1*2^{-3}$$

$$(110001{,}001)_2 = 32+16+1+0.125$$

$$(110001{,}001)_2 = (49.125)_{10}$$

b) What decimal value corresponds to the binary value 110001?

Please select an answer:

- 86
- 49
- 32

VIII.2.4.SUCCESSIVE DIVISION METHOD

The method of successive divisions consists of successively dividing by 2 the decimal number to be converted until the result of the division is a zero. The corresponding binary number will be the succession of remainders obtained. The most significant bit of this number is the remainder of the last division.

Example:

$(27)_{10}=(11011)_2$

27: 2 =	13: 2 =	6: 2 =	3: 2 =	1: 2 = 0
1	1	0	1	1

←

le reste de la dernière division sera écrit le premier (sens de lecture).

V III.2.5. SUCCESSIVE SUBTRACTIONS METHOD

To use this method, first determine the successive values of 2^i (i=0,...,n), then determine between which successive values of 2^i the number to be converted lies. The lower bound is then subtracted from the number. We proceed in the same way with the remainder obtained, until we obtain zero as the remainder of the subtraction.

The binary value will be 1 at the position of the weight used in the subtraction, and 0 at the position of the unused weights.

EXAMPLE

Using the method of successive subtractions, convert the decimal number $(230)_{10}$ in binary :

De	230	On peut retirer	128	reste	102	1
De	102	On peut retirer	64	reste	38	1
De	38	On peut retirer	32	reste	6	1
De	6	On ne peut pas retirer	16	reste	6	0
De	6	On ne peut pas retirer	8	reste	6	0
De	6	On peut retirer	4	reste	2	1
De	2	On peut retirer	2	reste	0	1
De	0	On ne peut pas retirer	1	reste	0	0

Sens de lecture

Le résultat est donc : $(230)_{10} = (11100110)_2$

V III.2.6.OCTAL SYSTEM

The octal system or base 8 has eight digits: 0, 1, 2, 3, 4, 5, 6, 7. The digits 8 and 9 do not exist in this base (B=8) Example :

Let's write down the numbers 45278 and 1274.6328 :

$$(4527)_8 = 4*8^3 + 5*8^2 + 2*8^1 + 7*8^0$$

$$(1274.632)_8 = 1*8^3 + 2*8^2 + 7*8^1 + 4*8^0 + 6*8^{-1} + 3*8^{-2} + 2*8^{-3}$$

V III.2.7.HEXADECIMAL SYSTEM

The use of base B =16 is a result of the development of microcomputers. The symbols used in this base are the ten digits from 0 to 9 completed by the letters A (for 10), B (for 11), C (for 12), D (for 13), E (for 14) and F (for 15).

Examples:

$$(4210)_{16} = 4*16^3 + 2*16^2 + 1*16^1 + 0*16^0$$

$$(2A4E)_{16} = 2*16^3 + 10*16^2 + 4*16^1 + 14*16^0$$

$$(C1B.D5)_{16} = 12*16^2 + 1*16^1 + 11*16^0 + 13*16^{-1} + 5*16^{-2}$$

Exercise

Convert the following binary numbers into hexadecimal: 1101, 10100111 and 01001011.

What binary value corresponds to the hexadecimal value 8E5?

Please choose an answer

- 1100 1110 0010
- 1111 0101 0101
- 1000 1110 0101
- 1000 0110 1010

VIII.2.8.ARITHMETIC OF NUMBERING SYSTEMS

Arithmetic operations are performed in any base B using the same methods as in base 10. A carry appears when the base B value is reached or exceeded.

> Addition

All you need to know is that :

0+0=0

0+1=1

1+0=1

1+1=0 Holding 1

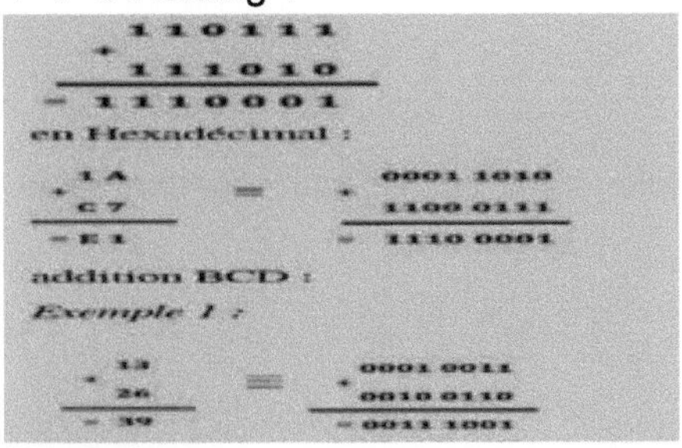

Example:

BCD addition :

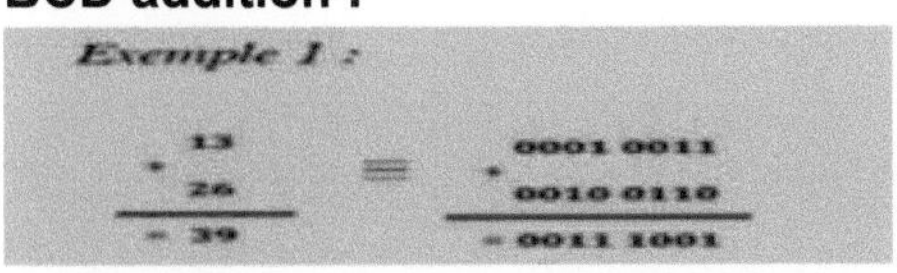

Example 2

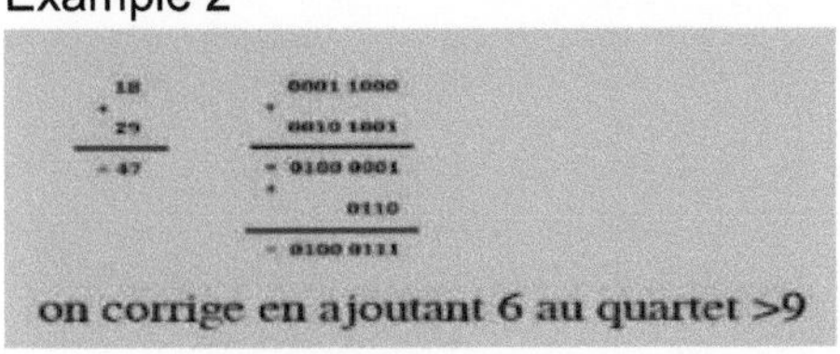

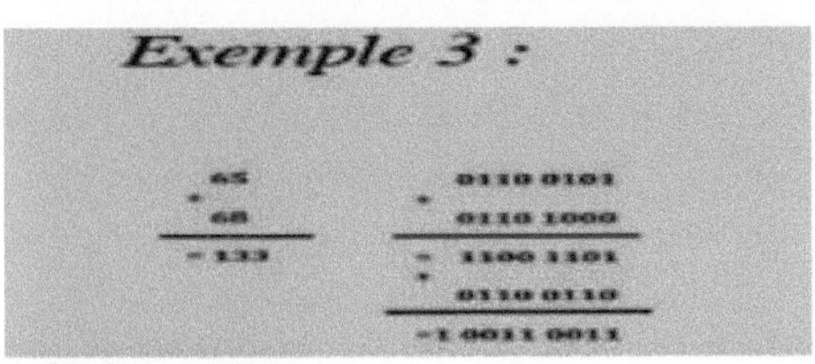

> Subtraction

All you need to know is that :

0-0=0

0-1=1 Report 1

1-0=1 1-1=0

Example:

10-9=+1

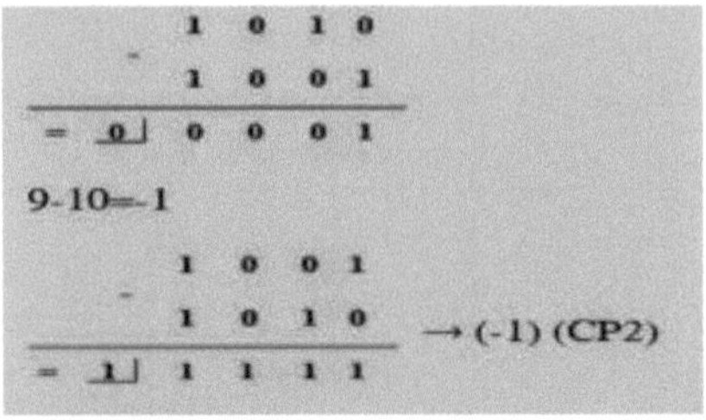

> Multiplication

Multiplication in binary is very simple, here is the multiplication table:
0x0=0 0x1=0
1x0=0 1x1=1

Example 1:
6x7=42

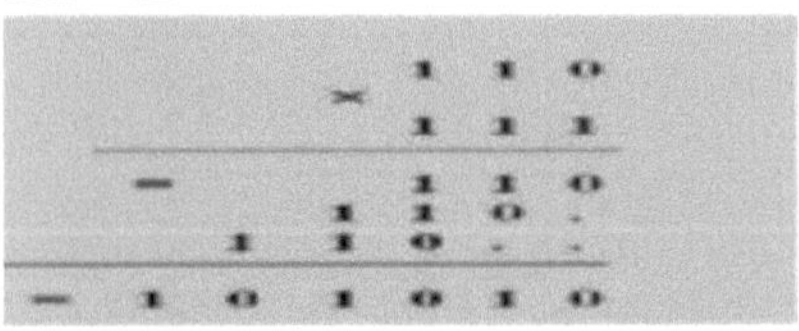

Example 2

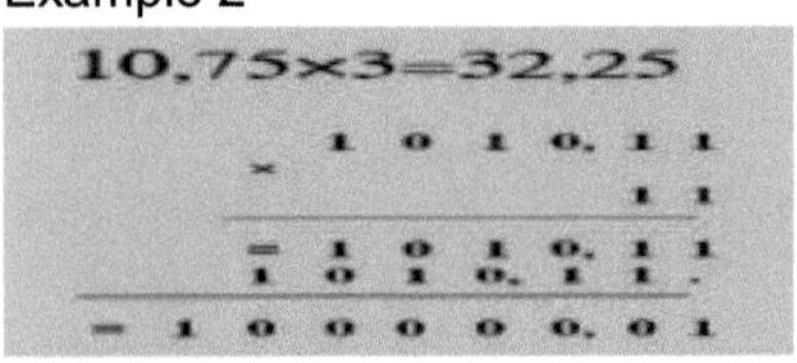

Exercise

What is the result of the following multiplication in binary :
1010*101

Please select an answer:

- 110010
- 110001
- 001101

> Division

The principle of binary division is similar to that of decimal division, but simpler in that each partial quotient is either equal to 1 (possible division) or 0 (impossible division). Division is the inverse operation of multiplication, in that one number is repeatedly subtracted from another until it is no longer possible, with a shift to the right each time.

The first step is to subtract the divisor from the dividend, starting from the left. If subtraction is not possible, the divisor is shifted one position to the right, after which subtraction is performed. The next subtraction takes place between the result of the previous subtraction, increased to the right of the next bit of the dividend according to the rule stated earlier. This step is repeated until all the bits of the dividend have been used up. For each subtraction, the result is written as 1, otherwise it is written as 0.

Example:

Make the following division:

42/7=6

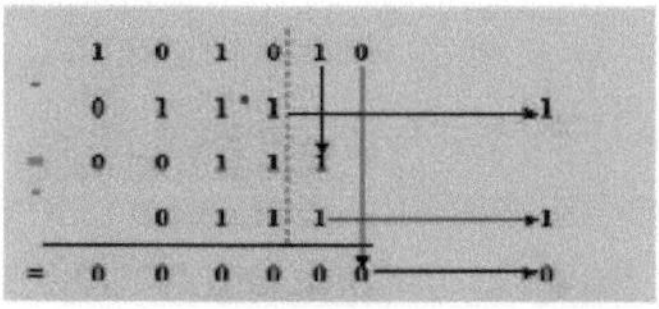

The result is therefore 110 with a remainder=0 (6 and remainder=0)

CHAPTER IX

BACKING UP COMPUTER DATA

IX.1. BASIC CONCEPTS

In general, a backup is a copy of data that can be used to restore the original after a loss of data. The purpose of creating a backup is to protect important files from loss due to hardware failure, software corruption, accidental deletion or other unforeseen disasters.

There are three types of backup: **full backup**, **incremental backup** and **differential backup**.

1) **Full backup**: A full backup copies all the files in the selected folders/directories to the specified destination. Full backups are generally performed less frequently than other types of backup because they require more time and storage space. If you have large amounts of data to back up, you may want to consider using an external hard drive or other removable storage device.

2) **Incremental backup**: An incremental backup copies only those files that have changed since the last (full or incremental) backup. Incremental backups are generally performed more frequently than full backups and require less time and storage space.

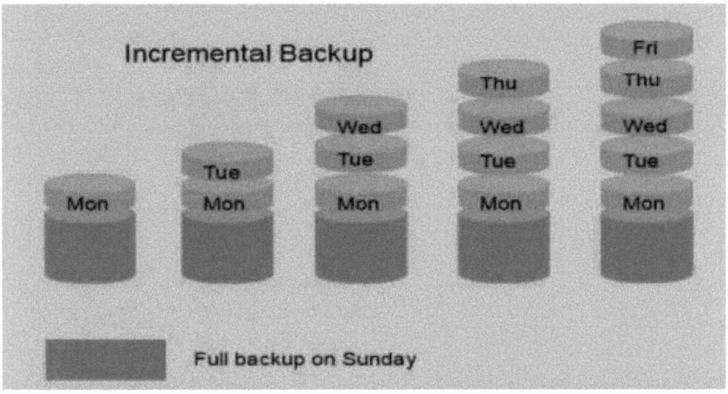

3) **Differential backup**: A differential backup copies only those files that have been modified since the last full backup. Differential backups are generally performed less frequently than incremental backups but more often than full backups. They require more time than incremental backups but less storage space.

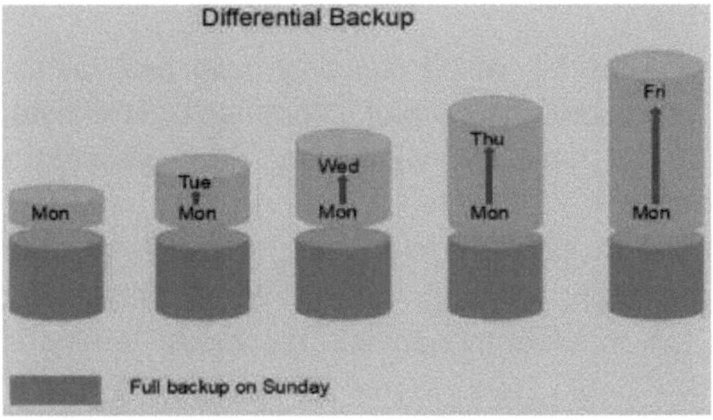

IX.2.MEASUREMENT UNIT AND ITS MULTIPLES

In the beginning was the bit. The bit is the smallest unit of measurement for digital information. It can only contain two values: 0 or 1. Very similar to the underlying electronics, it corresponds to a voltage or absence of voltage in the transistors.

Humans mainly use base 10 because they have ten fingers, making it easier for them to count in this base. In computing, base two - binary - has been chosen because it corresponds to the electronics used in computing. In fact, bit is the contraction **of Binary digIT**. It is symbolised by a lower-case "b".

Although the bit is the basic unit in computing, its small capacity - it can only contain 2 values - means that it cannot represent a significant amount of data on its own. Several bits are obviously needed to represent a meaningful value.

For example, in the early days of computing, most platforms used 7 and then 8 bits to encode alphabetic characters (plus numbers and punctuation) - *you can have a look at the commentaries for more details.*

It was therefore decided that groups of 8 bits would be better suited to representing the smallest amount of meaningful information - in this case a single character.

And so, on the 8th day, the byte was born. A byte is simply a group of 8 bits and represents the smallest quantity of information that the computer's components and peripherals (RAM, hard disks, etc.) work with.

The byte is therefore the unit with which we are most confronted when it comes to describing the size or capacity of digital information. A byte can represent 2^8, or 256 values, from 0 to 255 in decimal values. The byte symbol is the capital "B", or the "o" for octet in France.

Multiple

The smallest unit of value is the bit, which can only have two values, making it impossible to represent meaningful information. The byte, which is a group of 8 bits, can have 256 values and can represent a small amount of information.

There's no possible confusion between the two, because a 5Mb (megabyte) image is immediately 40Mb (megabit). Where things get complicated is when you talk in kilos, megabytes, gigabytes, terabytes and more.

In fact, the international system (SI) defines each of these prefixes as being worth 1000 times the previous one. So, in the metric system, 1km is equal to 1000m and so on.

In computing, on the other hand, as the base is base 2, the multiples must be multiples of 2, i.e. 1024 (2^{10}) and not 1000.

As this application of prefixes was not compatible with the SI, there were two standards: the SI prefixes (decimal) and the IEC prefixes (binary).

In order to differentiate between the two standards, each has its own notation.

Decimal			**Binary**		
Value	**SI prefix**		**Value**	**IEC prefix**	
1000	k	kilo	1024	Ki	Kibi
1000^2	M	mega	10242	Mi	Mebi
10003	G	giga	10243	Gi	Gibi
10004	T	tera	10244	Ti	Tebi
10005	P	peta	10245	Pi	Pebi
1000^6	E	exa	1024^6	Ei	Exbi
1000^7	Z	zetta	1024^7	Zi	Zebi
1000^8	Y	yotta	1024^8	Yi	Yobi

This is why, when you buy a 500GB (or Go) hard disk, it is *only* 467GiB when you connect it to Windows. This is because Windows chooses to display quantities according to the IEC standard, whereas hard drive manufacturers follow the SI convention for prefixes.

However, not all operating systems express quantities according to the IEC standard. MacOs for example, since version 10.6, displays the sizes of files, folders and peripherals with the decimal prefixes (SI). On a Mac, a 500GB disk is 500GB.

FIELDS OF APPLICATION

While in most cases (storage media size, transfer speed, etc.) SI prefixes prevail, memory size (cache and RAM) is always expressed as a binary value. For example, you might buy 1024 or 2048MB of RAM. This is less common nowadays, as systems are equipped with large amounts of RAM, so we talk in Giga without any further precision. Ex: "I have 16GB of RAM on my PC".

From the outset, we have spoken almost exclusively in terms of bytes. This is the smallest quantity of information with which peripherals work. However, there is one area in which bits are used more often than bytes: when we talk about transfer speed.

So when you download at 10Mb/s or 10Mbps (note the lower case "b"). You are therefore downloading at a speed of 1.25Mb/s. Don't be fooled!

That's all there is to it. Don't confuse bit and byte, one is worth 8 times as much as the other. And you need to be careful when choosing between decimal and binary notation. Especially as a lot of software displays MB when it's really MiB.

To obtain a rounded equivalent, multiply or divide (depending on the direction) by 1.05 for mega and 1.07 for giga. 500GB = 500/1.07 = 467.3GiB, which is the value we used in the hard disk example.

IX.3.OUTPUT ON SUPPORT

IX.3.1.EXTERNAL HARD DRIVE[4]

An external hard drive is extra storage space that lets you **keep your files,** back them up and keep them safe. To make sure you don't lose any of your data or multimedia files on your laptop or desktop computer , remember to back them up regularly on an external hard drive.

IX.3.1.1.OPERATION OF AN EXTERNAL HARD DRIVE

A simplified description of an external hard drive might look something like this: it's a giant USB stick. Plugged into a USB port on your computer, the external hard drive works in parallel with your main internal hard drive.

The **external hard drive** is installed in a hard drive enclosure connected to your computer. It is made up of several ceramic or metal discs,

[4] https://www.inmac-wstore.com, consulted on 05/10/2023 at 13h23'.

operating one on top of the other.
Electromagnets, or read/write heads, transmit or receive data by moving sideways. Using a converter, they transform the computer's language into a positive or negative magnetic field that polarises the surface of the disc over a defined area. The heads are thus raised and lowered at a precise point on the disc in an ultra-fast rotating movement.
When reading or writing is complete, the heads move into a safe position to prevent damage and protect the stored data.
There are now fully electronic external SSD disks which, although faster, are not yet capable of storing large quantities of data.

IX.3.2.USB KEY

A **USB flash drive** is a small removable medium that plugs into the USB port of a computer or, more recently, of certain hi-fi systems, DVD players, car radios, radio cassettes, television sets, etc. A USB flash drive contains a flash memory or mini hard drive. As it has no mechanical parts, it is highly resistant to shocks.

DESCRIPTION AND OPERATION

USB keys are powered by the USB port to which they are plugged, and unlike floppy disks, CDs or DVDs, they are impervious to dust and scratches, which is an advantage in terms of reliability. In 2008, the keys on the market are in USB 2.0 format. USB keys are relatively standardised, but some are not compatible with certain operating systems, requiring a driver to be installed.

CHARACTERISTICS

The USB Flash Drive has a number of features, detailed below.

- **Lifespan**

The lifetime (or MTBF) of the key itself is not specified and may fail after a few months or a few years, leading to partial or total loss of data.
Manufacturers claim that data will be retained for at least ten years, if not much longer. Computerworld is more cautious and draws attention to the major differences between different models in its article *Not all USB drives are created equal*. The reason for this is that the stored electrical charge representing the information is not perfectly insulated and can therefore disappear after a certain period of time, before which it must be rewritten to ensure that the data is retained; the quality of the insulation will therefore determine the retention time.
Do not confuse this retention period with the life of the key, which may break down or lose data long before this.
The loss of data can then be caused by :

- limited data retention, thanks to Flash Memory ;
- a breakdown of the key, like any other piece of equipment;
- a software problem in the operating system;
- a software manipulation error on the part of the user;
- a material handling error; it is not indestructible, although it is more resistant than other storage media.

- Performance

Performance depends very much on the design of the model, including the choice of components, architecture and memory controller. Techniques such as write amplification affect performance. Performance can also vary depending on the operating system or hardware on which it is used.

The data rate therefore varies for reading and writing, and also depends on the number of files copied and the way the contents of the key are organised. We can therefore have speeds of a few MB/s to several tens of MB/s, which can drop when transferring a large number of small files.

■ **Ergonomics**

There are a number of criteria to improve the ergonomics of the key: presence and positioning of the activity indicator light, connector protection system (rotating or retractable cap, retractable connector), accessories supplied (hand strap, necklace or chain, USB extension lead), portable software (encryption function, data synchronisation , email import, software suite), case design, etc.

IX.4.PRINT OUTPUT[5]

Output management includes all activities relating to the output of documents in print, e-mail or fax format. Form-based documents can be edited on an ad hoc basis or as part of a business process.

- **Ad hoc output** is generated when a user displays the preview of a document in Adobe® Reader and prints a hard copy or saves an

[5] https://help.sap.com, consulted on 06/10/2023 at 05h35'.

electronic copy of the document in PDF (Portable Document Format). This type of output requires no configuration and can be generated at any time.

• Process-integrated **output** means that the output of a document is automatically triggered and executed as part of a business process. Let's take the example of a purchase order created by an employee, then sent to his manager for approval. Once approved by the manager, the document is automatically sent to the output channel defined in the relevant editing options. This could be print, email or fax. Administrators can create output options and default output channel and form template rules to define how a particular document is automatically output.

CHAPTER X

NETWORK

X.1.BASIC CONCEPTS

X.1.1.DEFINITION

The computer network refers to interconnected computer devices that can exchange data and share resources with each other .[6]

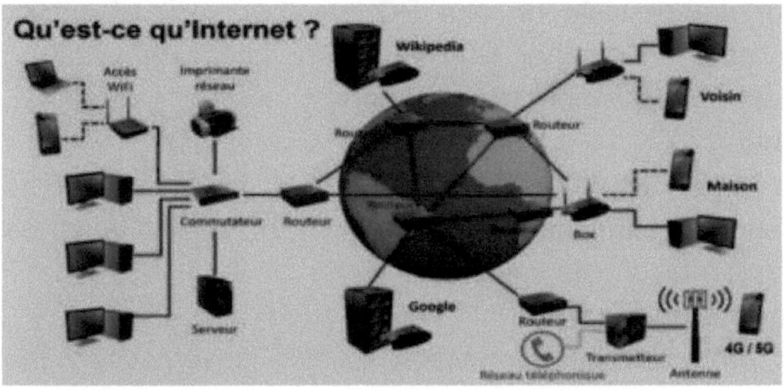

X.1.2.ADVANTAGES AND DISADVANTAGES

a) BENEFITS[7]

- **Central data storage**

Files can be stored on a central node (the file server) which can be shared and made available to all users in an organisation.

- **Anyone can connect to a computer network**

The range of skills required to connect to a modern computer network is negligible. The ease of connection means that even young children can start to exploit the data.

[6] https://aws.amazon.com, consulted on 06/10/2023 at 05h38'.
[7] https://www.phpeasydata.com, consulted on 06/10/2023 at 05h50'.

- **Faster problem resolution**

Because an in-depth procedure is broken down into a number of smaller procedures, each of which is handled by all the associated gadgets, an explicit question can be answered in less time.

- **Reliability**

Reliability means safeguarding information. If for any reason information is compromised or inaccessible on one PC, another copy of similar information is available on another workstation for later use, allowing further work and processing without interruption.

- **It is very flexible**

This innovation is known for being really adaptable, because it offers customers the chance to examine everything from the basics, such as programming, without affecting its usefulness.

- **Security through authorisation**

The security and protection of information is also governed by the system. As only clients of the system are authorised to access specific files or applications, no other person can breach the protection or security of the information.

- **It increases storage capacity**

As you will be sharing data, files and assets with others, you need to ensure that all information and substance is legitimately stored within the framework. With this innovation in systems administration, you can do most of this work with ease, while still having plenty of room for capacity.

b) DISADVANTAGES[8]

- **Safety concerns**

One of the main drawbacks of computer networks is the security problems associated with them. If a computer is stand-alone, physical access becomes necessary for any type of data theft. However, if a computer is on a network, a hacker can gain unauthorised access using a variety of tools. In the case of large organisations, various network security software packages must be used to prevent the theft of any confidential and classified data.

- **Viruses and malware**

If only one computer in a network is affected by a virus, there is a possible threat that other systems will also be affected. Viruses can spread easily across a network, due to the inter-connectivity of workstations. In addition, multiple systems with shared resources are a breeding ground for viruses. Similarly, if malicious software is

[8] https://www.codyx.org, consulted on 06/10/2023 at 06h02'.

accidentally installed on the central server, all network clients connected to this server will automatically be affected.

- **Lack of robustness**

If the main file server in a computer network fails, the whole system becomes useless. If y a central link server or bridging device in the network, and it fails, the whole network comes to a standstill. In the case of large networks, the file server must be a powerful computer, which often makes setting up and maintaining the system doubly expensive.

- **Need for an efficient manager**

The technical skills and know-how required to operate and administer a computer network are considerably high. Any user with only basic skills cannot do the job. What's more, the responsibility that goes with such a job is high, since assigning usernames-passwords and authorisations to network users are also the tasks of the network administrator. Similarly, connecting and configuring the
are also tedious tasks, and cannot be carried out by the average user who does not have advanced computer and/or network skills.

- **Lack of independence**

Since most networks have a centralised server and dependent clients, client users lack complete freedom. Centralised decision-making can sometimes get in the way of the way a client user wants to use their own computer. Computer networks have had a profound effect on the way we communicate with each other today, and have made our lives easier.

From the World Wide Web to the local area network in your office, computers have become an indispensable part of everyday life, and networks have become a norm in most businesses. If networks are designed and configured with their advantages and disadvantages in mind, they are the best installation you can have.

X.1.3.CHARACTERISTICS OF A COMPUTER NETWORK[9]

A network has a number of characteristics that define its behaviour and performance. These characteristics are as follows:

- **Topology**: The physical or logical arrangement of devices and links in a network. The topology can be a bus, a star, a ring, a mesh or a hybrid, depending on the network configuration.
- **Protocol**: The rules and standards that govern communication between devices on a network. The protocol may be TCP/IP, HTTP, FTP, SMTP or other, depending on the type of data being transmitted.
- **Bandwidth**: the capacity of the network to transmit data, measured in

[9] https://commentouvrir.com, consulted on 06/10/2023 at 06h12'.

bits per second (bps), kilobits per second (Kbps) or megabits per second (Mbps). Bandwidth can be shared or dedicated, depending on the network architecture.

- **Latency**: The delay or lag in the transmission of data between devices on a network, measured in milliseconds (ms) or microseconds (ps). Latency can be affected by factors such as distance, congestion or processing time.
- **Security**: The measures and protocols that guarantee the confidentiality, integrity and availability of data in a network. Security may include authentication, encryption, firewalls or intrusion detection systems.

X.1.4.TYPES OF COMPUTER NETWORKS[10]

X.1.4.1. LAN NETWORK

LAN stands for *Local Area Network.* This is a set of computers belonging to the same organisation and linked together in a small geographical area by a network, often using the same technology (the most widespread being Ethernet)...

A local area network is therefore a network in its simplest form. The data transfer speed? of a local network can range from 10 Mbps (for an ethernet network, for example) to 1 Gbps (in FDDI or Gigabit Ethernet, for example). The size of a local network can be up to 100 or even 1000 users.

X.1.4.2. MAN NETWORK

MANs (*Metropolitan Area Networks*) interconnect several geographically close LANs (no more than a few dozen km apart) at high speeds . A MAN allows two distant nodes to communicate as if they were part of the same local network.

A MAN is made up of switches or routers interconnected by high-speed links (usually fibre optics).

X.1.4.3. WAN NETWORK

A **WAN** (Wide Area Network) interconnects several LANs across large geographical distances.

The speeds available on a WAN are the result of a trade-off with the cost of the links (which increases with distance) and can be low.

WANs use routers to "choose" the most appropriate route to reach a network node.

The best-known WAN is the Internet

[10] https://web.maths.unsw.edu.au, consulted on 06/10/2023 at 06h26'.

X.1.5.INTRANET NETWORK[11]

An intranet is a local network specific to an organisation (company, university, institution, etc.) that enables employees to access internal information and exchange information. It works like a website: it requires a web server and the associated protocols.

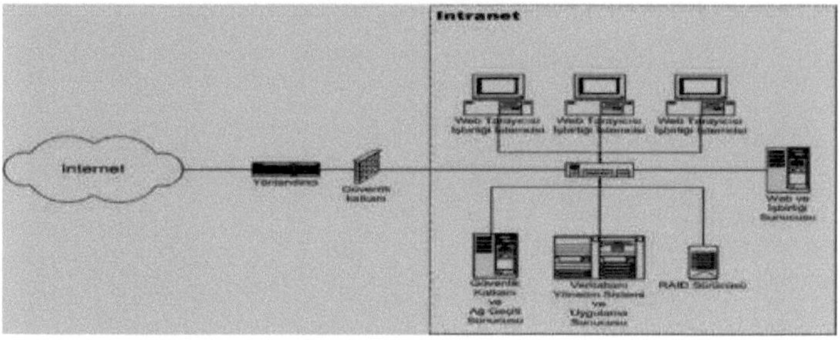

X.1.6.EXTRANET NETWORK[12]

The **extranet** is an extension of the company's information system. It is based on a telecommunications network linked to the Internet, enabling all companies to share documents or private information with their employees, subsidiaries, customers, suppliers or service providers. For example, employees working from home can connect to a web interface with their login and password to retrieve this information.

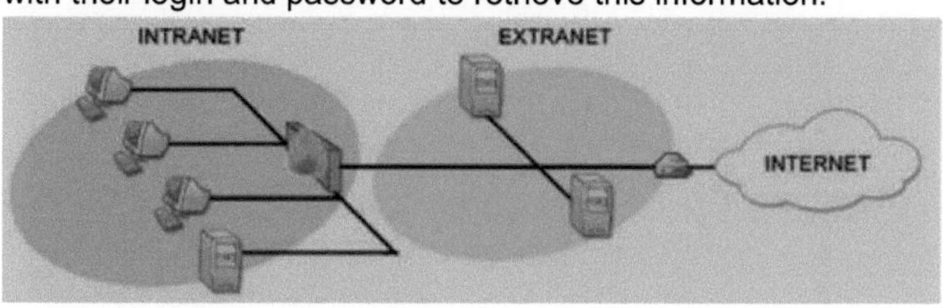

X.1.7.INTERNET NETWORK

The Internet is a worldwide computer network that enables users to communicate with each other across the globe at a very low cost, since all you need is a simple connection. [13]

[11] https://blog.talkspirit.com, consulted on 06/10/2023 at 06h32'.
[12] http://www.saveho.com, consulted on 06/10/2023 at 06h45'.
[13] https://www.futura-sciences.com, consulted on 06/10/2023 at 06:52'.

CHAPTER XI

ELECTRONIC MAIL

XI.1.DEFINITION

Electronic *mail* refers to the service of transferring messages sent by an electronic messaging system *via* a computer network (now the Internet) to the electronic mailbox of a recipient chosen by the sender. "Correspondence service enabling electronic messages to be exchanged via a computer network. "[14]

Email, a contraction of the words **courrier** and **electronique**, also refers to the message exchanged by this means according to the official terminology in the French language .[15]

XI.2.CREATING AN E-MAIL ADDRESS

First, choose a Google Account type

This account will be for me or for running a business

NB: When you create a Google Account for your business, you can activate personalisation for businesses. A Business Account also makes it easier to configure the Google business listing, which helps to improve the visibility of your business and manage your information online.

When you create a Google Account, you'll be asked for personal information. By providing accurate information, you'll help keep your account secure and make our services more useful to you.

Also if you don't need a Gmail account to create a Google Account. You can use an email address other than Gmail to create one.

1. Go to the Google Account login page.
2. Click on Create an account.
3. Enter your name.
4. In the "User name" field, enter a user name.
5. Enter your password and confirm.

NB: When you enter your mobile password, the first letter is not case-sensitive.

6. Click Next.

- Optional: Add a telephone number to your account, then validate .

7. Click Next.

USE AN EXISTING E-MAIL ADDRESS

1. Go to the Google Account login page.
2. Click on Create an account.
3. Enter your name.

[14] https://www.techno-science.net, consulted on 06/10/2023 at 07:04'.

[15] Ditto

4. Click on Use my current e-mail address instead.
5. Enter your current e-mail address.
6. Click Next.
7. Validate your e-mail address using the code sent to your existing e-mail address.
8. Click on Validate.

XI.3.CREATING A YAHOO ADDRESS

To **create a yahoo.fr email address**, go to the **Yahoo** home page from your browser.

1. Go to the Yahoo login page or type the URL login.yahoo.com
2. Click on the "Create an account" button at the bottom right of the page.
3. Fill in the required information: first name, surname, telephone number, gender, date of birth, etc. Fields marked with an asterisk are mandatory. Choose an **e-mail address** and a strong password to protect your personal data.

XI .4.CREATING A HOTMAIL ADDRESS

Since Hotmail became Outlook.com, it's become less easy to create an account. If you already have an internet address *@hotmail.fr*, *@hotmail.com* or *@msn.com*, you will automatically be redirected to the login.live.com address, which leads to the new Outlook version of the Hotmail mailbox.

Here are a few simple steps to access this amazing mail service.

1. You'll need to visit **outlook.com**.
2. The next thing you need to do is click on the "Create a free account" button at the bottom, which will take you to the registration page.
3. When you receive a new e-mail address, you will then be able to choose your domain name, i.e. *@outlook.fr* or *@hotmail.fr.*

Enter

4. You will need to enter a username and password, which will now be

used to **access Hotmail**. Microsoft will then ask you whether or not you want to receive promotional emails. You will then choose whether or not you wish to receive promotional emails from Microsoft.

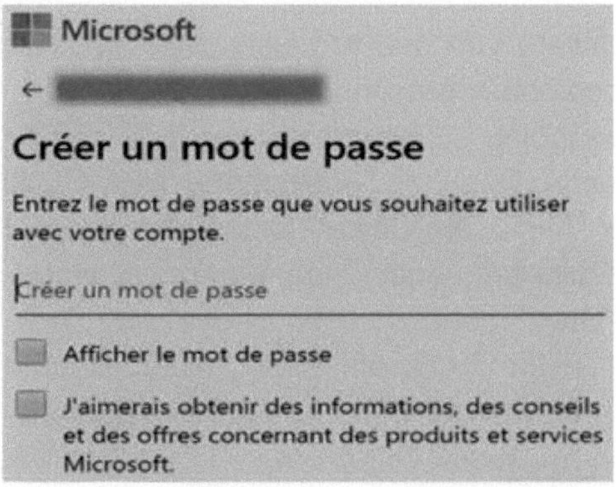

5. Microsoft will then ask you for some important information such as your name, your date of birth, your gender, your telephone number in case you forget your password, your place of residence... Of course, Hotmail guarantees the protection of your data
6. Next, Microsoft will probably ask you to confirm that you are not a robot by entering the characters you see.

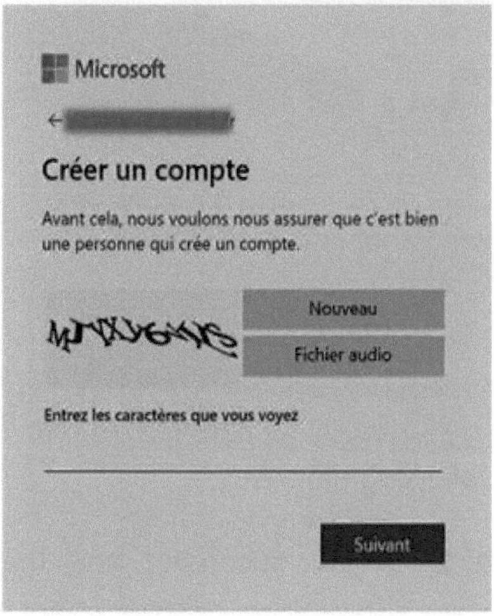

7. Once you've entered your details, you'll need to click on your request and confirm it, which will be the last step in **obtaining the Hotmail account**.
8. Click and confirm. Verification will be sent to you by text or email to ensure that **your Hotmail account is created** and in safe hands.

CHAPTER XII

POWERPOINT PRESENTATION

XII .1.POWERPOINT LAUNCH

Microsoft PowerPoint is the software you use to create, edit and view rich multimedia slideshows to accompany presentations and lectures.

All you need to do is launch Powerpoint:

1. Using the Windows "Start" menu. Open the "Start" menu, click on "All Programs", scroll down to the "Microsoft Office" folder and click on "PowerPoint". If you use PowerPoint frequently, the program will appear on the right when you open the "Start" menu, so keep an eye on it there.
2. Open Microsoft PowerPoint in the "Program Files" folder. Double-click on the "My Computer" icon on the desktop, "Local Disk (C:)", then "Program Files" . Double-click on "Microsoft Office", then "PowerPoint" to launch the program
3. Locate your presentation folder - which appears in "ppt" format. - And open it by launching Microsoft PowerPoint. Access your folder, probably stored in your "Documents" library, then double-click on it to open it using PowerPoint.

XII.2.DESCRIPTION OF THE WINDOW

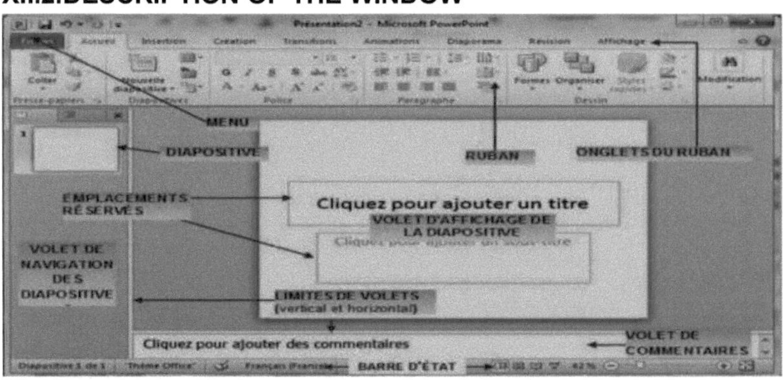

The Powerpoint window consists of the following elements:

1. **THE TITLE BAR** displays the name of the document and the application (Powerpoint) ;
2. **THE FILE MENU** provides global commands for document management;
3. **THE "QUICK ACCESS" TOOL BAR** displays icons which symbolise the most common actions (tools);
4. **THE SCROLL**, made up of tabs, displays icons grouped by type, symbolising actions;

5. **THE NAVIGATION PANE** displays the map or slides of the presentation;

6. **RESERVED SPACES**, characterised by icons, describe the type of element (graphic, image, table, etc.);

7. **CONTEXTUAL MENUS AND TOOLBARS** offer the most appropriate tools and commands for a current selection;

8. **THE LIFTS** allow you to move vertically and horizontally with the mouse;

9. **THE STATUS BAR** gives information about the current command, the environment and the position of the insertion point (the display icons and zoom allow you to switch from one display mode and/or magnification to another);

10. **THE DISPLAY PANE** displays the slide and its components ■ ■ ■ ;

11. **THE COMMENTS PANE** completes the display pane .

XII.3.DESIGN COMPONENT

1) You can request design ideas at any time by selecting Design > Designer  in the Ribbon.

2) The first time you try it out Designer may ask your permission to get design ideas for you.

If you wish to use the Designer, select **Activate**.

Once you have enabled "connected experiences", PowerPoint design ideas are automatically presented to you when you create your slides. Over time PowerPoint learns from your experience of using design ideas and shows you design ideas when you need them.

3) Browse the suggestions in the **Designer** pane on the right of the window;

4) Click on the design of your choice or close the window. If you select one of the ideas, your slide will be modified accordingly.

You can also select another idea in the pane or return to the original design of your slide: Press Ctrl+Z to cancel a design you have just selected.

XII.4.AVAILABLE RIBBONS

All the new menu structure is now in a 'ribbon' of commands. This part of the document is intended to give you an overview of the new way of accessing commands.

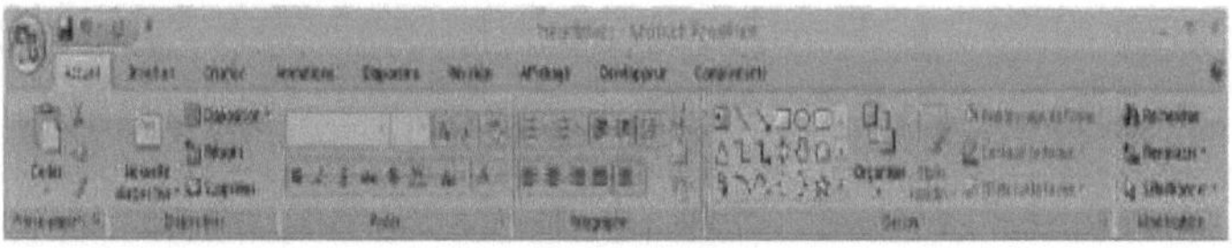

The ribbon can take up a lot of screen space. You can double-click the active tab to show or hide the ribbon.

Office button

The Office button groups together most of the commands that were previously in the File menu. It also contains the options for managing the application.

Quick access bar

Microsoft recognises that are certain commands that you will use more than others. That's why it lets you customise the toolbar to suit your needs.

To add or remove options from the quick access bar

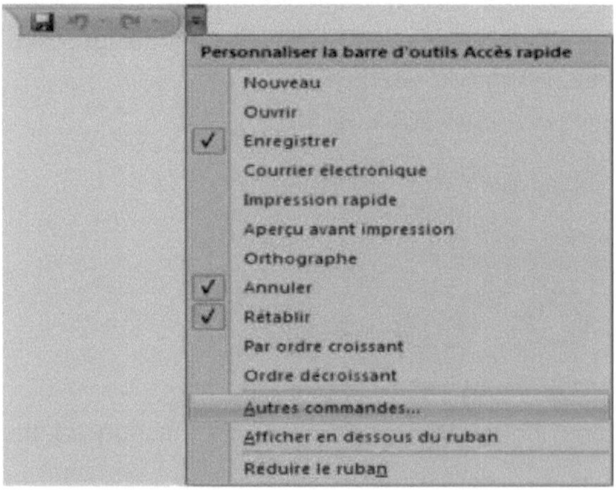

1) Press the downward-pointing arrow at the end of the Quick Access toolbar.

You can activate the most frequently used commands.
2) To access additional commands, select the option
Other orders.

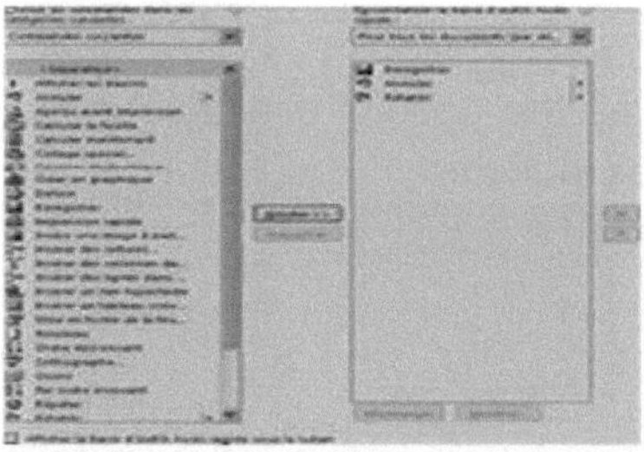

The tabs

It is under these tabs that you will find the commands that make up PowerPoint. They are in the order that you should use to create your presentation. There's nothing to stop you switching from one tab to another at any time. But remember to look at them all before you've completed your document.

Contextual tabs

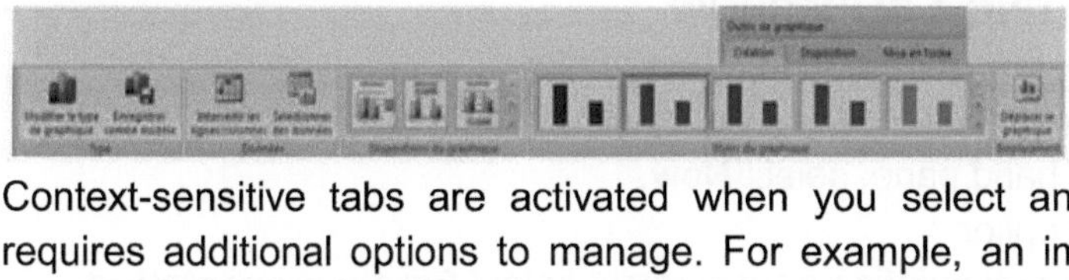

Context-sensitive tabs are activated when you select an object that requires additional options to manage. For example, an image, graph, diagram or video is not managed in the same way as text. A tab will be added after the other tabs to provide options for the object you have selected. In the case of graphics such as the image above, there are so many options that they are grouped under three tabs: Creation, Layout and Formatting .

Option group: grouping of orders

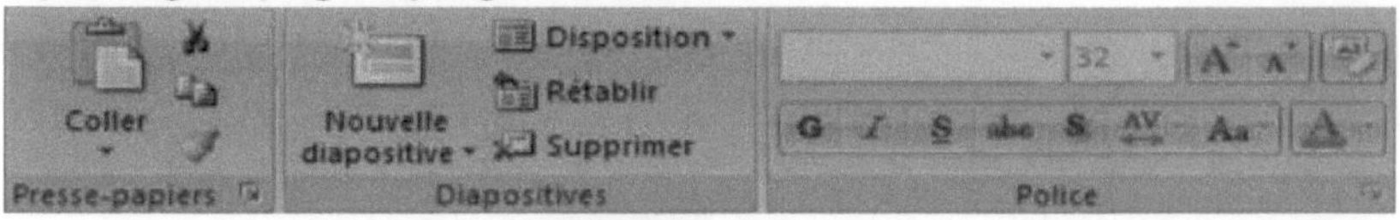

The commands are grouped together to cover all similar options. In the image above, there is the clipboard group which includes the Cut, Copy, Paste and Reproduce presentation style commands. There are also groupings for commands that cover options for slides and fonts.

Orders

These are the commands that allow you to modify your documents to better suit your needs.

Dialog box launcher

The ribbon is not big enough to cover all the options available in the applications. That's why y has a dialog box launcher.

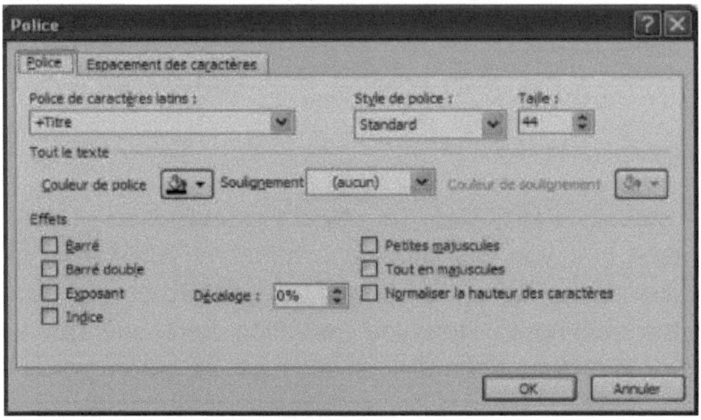

XII.5.FIRST SLIDE SHOW

XII.5.1.CREATING A SLIDESHOW

Here are the steps for creating a slideshow;

1. Open PowerPoint.
2. In the left-hand pane, select **New**.
3. Select an option :

- To create a presentation from scratch, select **Empty presentation**.
- To use a prepared design, select one of the models.
- To display tips on using PowerPoint, select

Guided tour, then **Creer**.

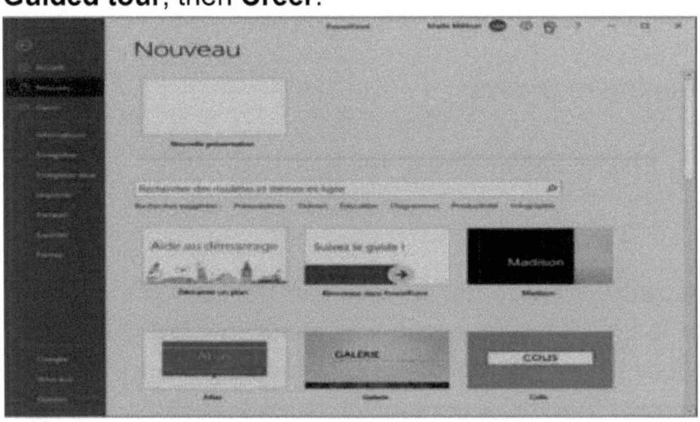

ADD A SLIDE

1. In the thumbnails in the left-hand pane, select the slide you want your new slide to follow.
2. On the **Home** tab, in the **Slides** section, select **New slide**.
3. In the **Slides** section, select **Layout**, then select the desired layout from the menu.

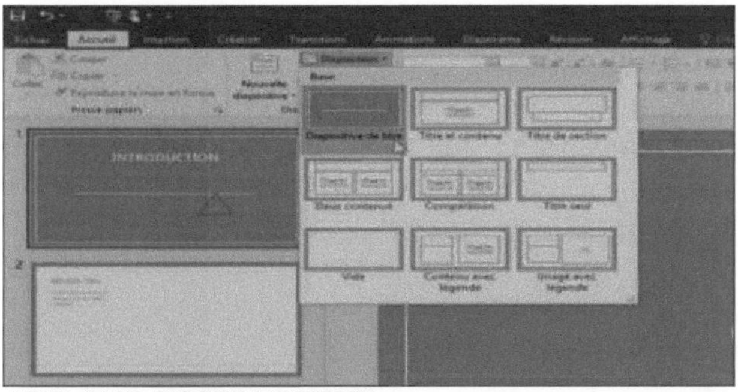

ADD AND FORMAT TEXT

1. Place the cursor inside a text box, then type something .
2. Select the text, then select one or more options in the **Font** section of the **Home** tab, such as **Font**, **Increase font size**, **Decrease font size**, **Bold**, **Italic**, **Underline**, etc.
3. To create bulleted or numbered lists, select the text, then select the **Bullets** or **Numbering** option.

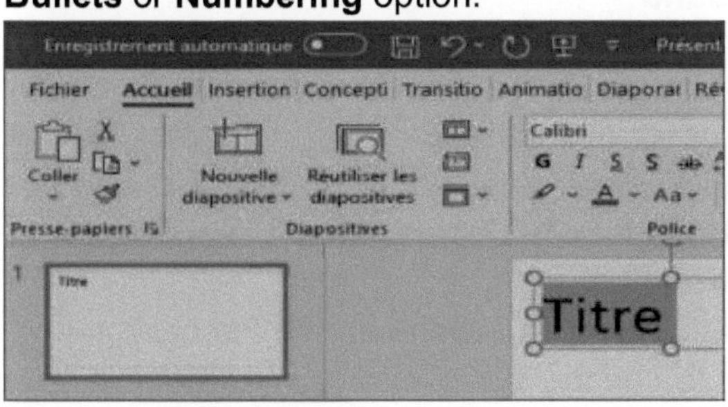

ADD AN IMAGE, SHAPE, ETC.

1. Go to the **Insert** tab.
2. To add an image :
   - In the **Images** section, select **Images**.
   - In the **Insert an image from** menu, select the desired source.
   - Find the image you want, select it and then **select Insert**.
3. To add illustrations :

o In the **Illustrations** section, select **Shapes**, **Icons**, **3D Models**, **Smart Art** or **Graphics**.

o In the dialogue box that opens when you click on one of the illustration types, select the desired element and follow the prompts to insert it.

XII.5.2.BACKGROUNDS

To create a watermark in PowerPoint (2007), follow these steps:

Step 1. Open the PowerPoint file

Go to the PowerPoint document whose background you want to change, and click on the "Design" > "Format background" button. If you are using PowerPoint 2007, you can go to the "Design" tab and click on "Background styles".

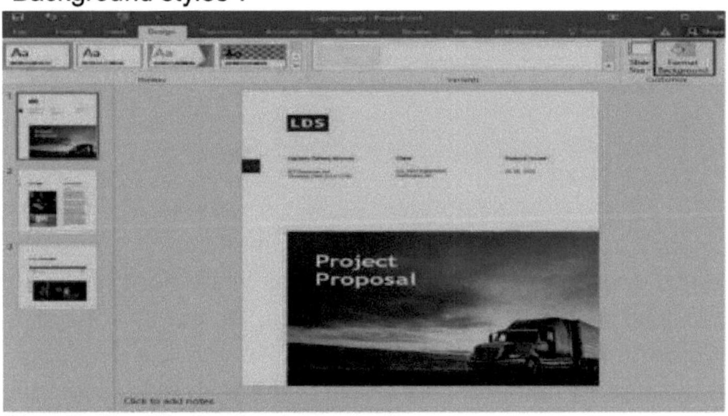

Step 2. Modify the background

A new window opens. Select the "Solid fill" option and click on the "Colour" icon. A wide choice of options appears. Simply click on the colour you want to fill the background with. You can also choose to use gradients or images as the background.

Step 3. Modify the background

There are also a few alternatives you can use to modify the background. Drag the transparency filter to change the level of transparency in your document. You can also click on the "Apply to all" option to set the background colour for all the slides.

XII.5.3.USE OF MASKS

A slide **mask** is the top slide in a slide hierarchy which stores information about the theme and layout of the slides in a presentation, including background, colour, fonts, effects, size of placeholders and positioning.[16]
To use several themes in the same presentation, you need to use several slide masks. Each slide mask represents a theme.
For example, the following image shows two slide masks (with associated layouts below each) as they appear in Slide Mask mode. A different theme is applied to each slide mask.

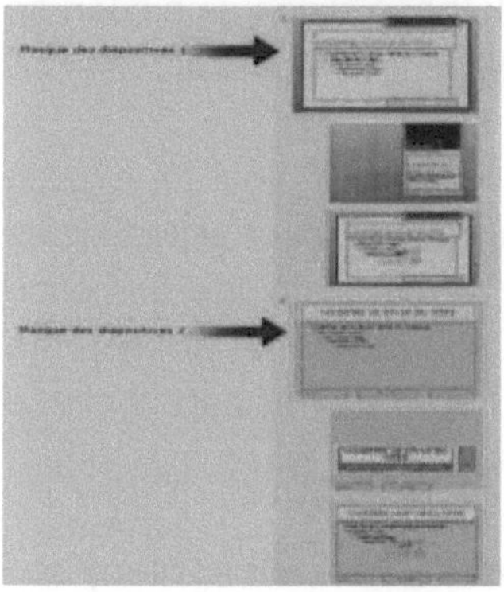

ADDING AN ADDITIONAL SLIDE MASK TO A PRESENTATION

1. In the **View** tab, click on **Mask slides**.
2. In the **Slide mask** tab, perform one of the following operations:

- In the **Modify master page** group, click **Insert slide mask**.

When you use this procedure to insert a slide mask, it appears under an existing mask and without theme colours or effects. You can apply a

[16] https://support.microsoft.com, consulted on 11/10/2023 at 02:54'.

custom theme using the options in the **Background** group.

- Under the **Slide mask** tab, in the **Edit theme** group, click **Themes**, then select a new theme.

If your presentation contains only one slide mask, selecting a new theme using this procedure will replace the existing theme in the mask with the new theme.

XII.5.4.VIEWING A SLIDESHOW

If you are in Slideshow mode and decide to display a hidden slide, you can do so:

1. Right-click on the active slide and **select Show all slides**.

The screen switches to a thumbnail list of all the slides in the presentation.

2. Select the hidden slide to display.

The selected slide is displayed in full screen and the slideshow resumes.

If you're using Presenter mode, your audience won't see the steps you take to select the slide. They will simply see the slide you select in step 2.

WHY HIDE THE SLIDES?

Hiding slides is particularly useful when you have added slides to a presentation which provide different levels of detail on the subject, perhaps for different audiences. You can mark these slides as hidden so that they are not displayed in your main slideshow, but you can still access them if required.

For example, a member of your audience may ask you to explain something in more detail. In this case, you can reveal the masked slides that contain these details. However, if time is short and the audience understands the concepts you are providing, you may wish to keep the slides with the additional information masked so that you can continue your presentation without visibly ignoring the slides.

XII.5.5.INTERRUPTING A SLIDESHOW

For the types of slideshow **Presented by a presenter (full screen)** and **Viewed on a terminal (full screen)**, it may be useful to check and record the timing of effects and slides.

1. In the **Slideshow** tab, click **Check timing**.

Note: The presentation timer starts as soon as you click on **Check Timing**.

The **Repeat** toolbar is displayed and the timing of the presentation begins in the **Duration** area **of the slide**.

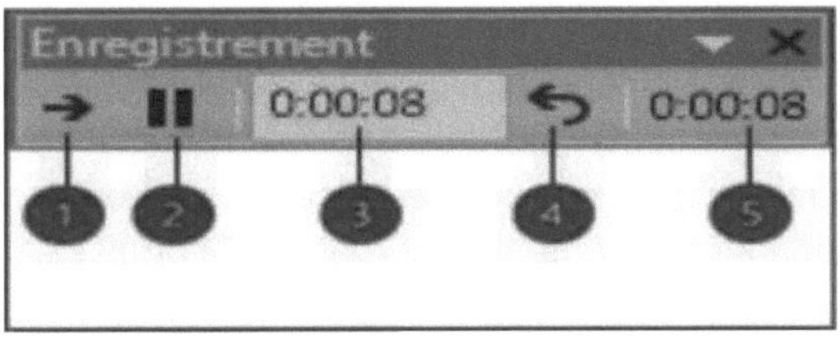

oNext (advances to the next slide)
"Pause
3Duree of the slide
-♦Repeter
©Total length of slideshow
2. While the presentation is being timed, you can use the **Repeat** toolbar to perform one or more of the following operations:

- To move on to the next slide, click **Next.**
- To stop recording temporarily, click on **Suspend**.
- To resume recording the duration after pausing, click **Pause**.
- To set the exact display time for a slide, enter the corresponding value in the **Slide time** field.
- To resume recording for the duration of the active slide, click **Repeat**.

3. Once the duration of the last slide has been set, a message displays the total duration of the presentation and prompts you to perform one of the following operations:

- To keep the timings of the recorded slides, click **Yes.**
- To delete the timings from the saved slides, click **No.**

Slide sorter mode is activated and displays the duration of each slide in your presentation.

XII.6.TRANSITIONS

A transition is an animated effect that occurs when you move from one slide to the next [1718] .

XII.6.1.APPLICATION OF A TRANSITION [18]

To apply a transition effect to all the slides in the presentation, press the "Apply everywhere" button.

The "Go to next slide" option lets you decide how to move to the next slide. You can do this manually by clicking on the left mouse button or by

[17] https://www.onlyoffice.com, consulted on 11/10/2023 at 03h19'.
[18] https://lecompagnon.info, consulted on 11/10/2023 at 03h32'.

using certain keys. But you can also advance automatically after a certain amount of time. This is very useful for "carousel" type presentations; which repeat continuously without any intervention. You see them on screens in shopping centres or in front of buildings. You can determine how long each slide stays on the screen before automatically moving on to the next.

Transition sound

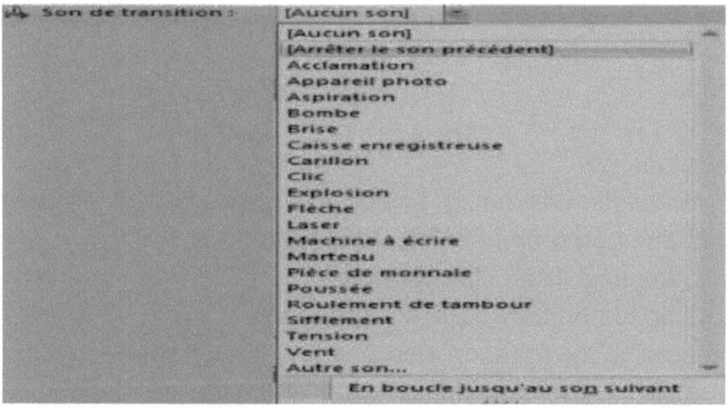

Transition speed

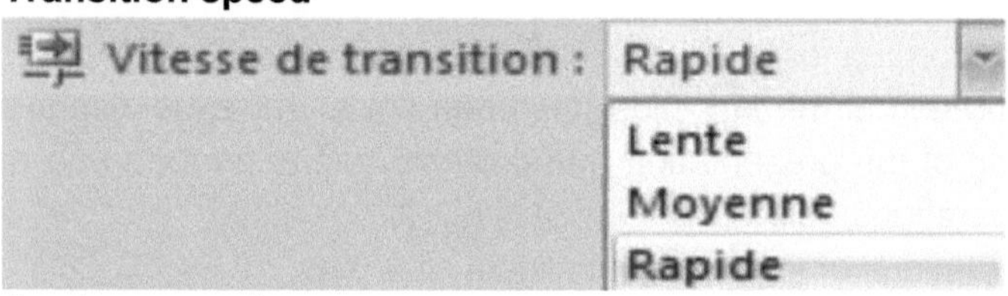

Apply everywhere

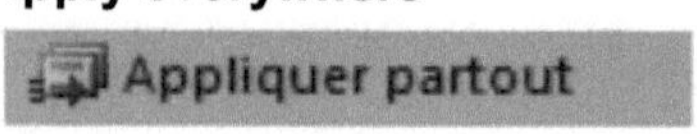

Go to next slide

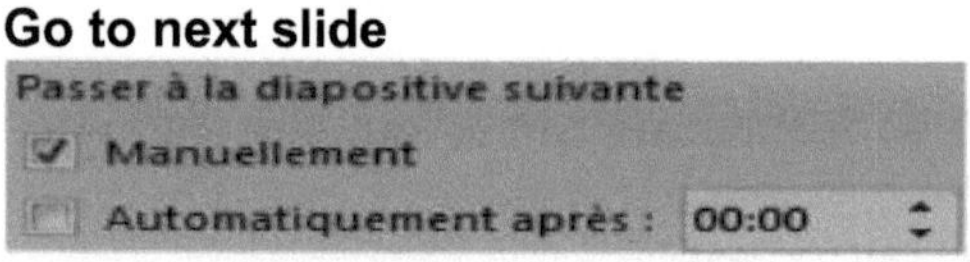

XII.6.2.PREVIEWING EFFECTS

1. On the slide, select the area containing your text.
2. Select **the Animations tab,** then choose an animation, for example **Appearance, Fade** in or **Appearance.**

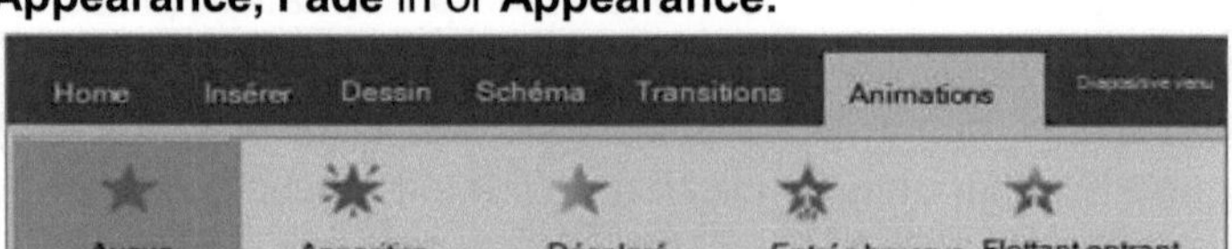

For some animations, such as the line feed, select Effect **options**, as

you need to choose a direction for the bullet feed (down, up, left or right).
3. Select **Effect Options,** then **Select By** Paragraph to display the paragraphs of text one at a time. (The other option, **All at once**, makes all the lines of text appear at once).

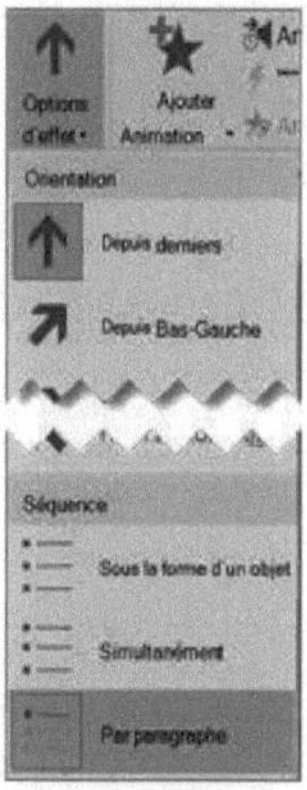

PowerPoint immediately previews the animation for you.

By default, when you present a slideshow, each paragraph is displayed in response to a click. This allows you to control the appearance of each paragraph. You can change this setting using the **Start,** Duration and Delay controls at the far right of the Ribbon **Animation** tab.

XII.6.3.SETTING THE TRANSITION TIME[19]

To change the duration of specific transitions in a project :

1. In the project browser, double-click on the transition icon. (There are many transition style icons; several are shown below).

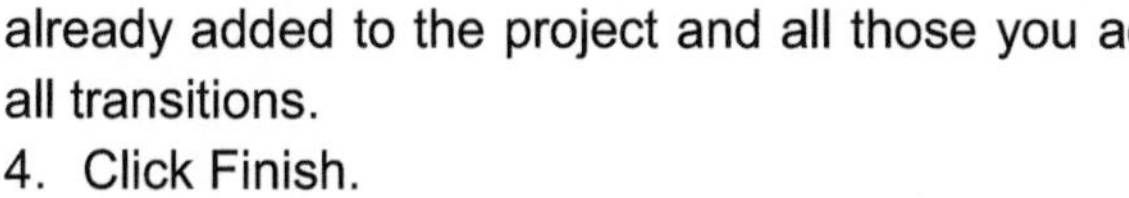

2. In the inspector that opens, enter the number of seconds you want the transition to last.
3. If you want this duration to be applied to all the transitions you have already added to the project and all those you add later, select Apply to all transitions.
4. Click Finish.

To change the default duration of transitions in a project :

1. When your project is open, choose File > Project properties.

The File menu appears in a light grey bar at the top of your computer screen.

[19] https://imovie.skydocu.com, consulted on 11/10/2023 at 03h48'.

2. Move the "Transition duration" slider to define the duration, in seconds, of transitions without a theme.
3. Similarly, move the "Theme transition length" slider to define the length, in seconds, of the theme transitions.
If this cursor is white and does not move, this means that your project has no theme.
4. Select one of the following options:
- Apply to all transitions, if you want the settings to apply to all transitions, y including all the transitions you have already added and all those you are going to add from now on.
- Apply when added to the project, if you want the settings to apply simply to the transitions you add from that point onwards.

5. Click OK.

XII .6.4.AUTOMATIC OPERATION

You can use an auto-run presentation to run unassisted on a stand or kiosk at a trade show or convention, or you can record it as a video and send it to a customer.

1. On the **Slideshow** tab, click **Configure slideshow**.
2. Under **Slideshow type**, choose one of the following options:

- So that the person watching your slideshow can switch from one slide to another whenever they like, click on **Presented by a presenter (full screen)**.
- To present your slideshow in a window (where the person viewing the presentation has no control over the progress of the slideshow), select **Viewed by a person (window)**.
- To run your slideshow in a loop until the viewer presses Esc, select **View on a terminal (full screen)**.

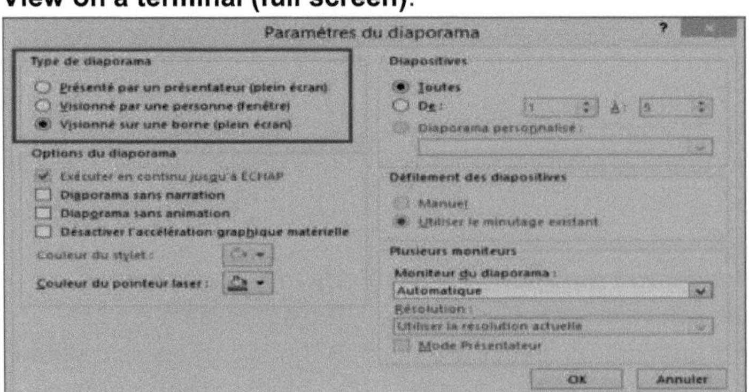

XII.7 DISPLAY MODE[20]

By default, PowerPoint opens in Normal mode, displaying thumbnails, notes and Slide mode. If you prefer, however, you can specify that PowerPoint opens in another mode, such as Slide Sorter, Slide Show, Notes Page and variations on Normal mode.

1. Click on **File>** **Options>** **Advanced options**.
2. Under **View,** in the Open all **documents** using this view list, select the view you want to set as the new default view, then click **OK.**

[20] https://diapo-powerpoint.com, consulted on 11/10/2023 at 03h58'.

CHAPTER XIII

IT SYSTEMS ADMINISTRATION AND SECURITY

XIII.1.DEFINITIONS OF CONCEPTS

1) Administration (in IT): managing and ensuring the functioning and operation of one or more hardware or software elements (tools, networks, databases, messaging, etc.) in a company or organisation. Ensures that information is consistent, accessible and secure .[21]

2) Security (in IT) : IT security is a general term used to describe all the strategies, methods, solutions and tools used to protect the confidentiality, integrity and availability of a company's data and digital resources .[22]

3) Computer systems: A computer system is a set of computer and telecommunications resources, both hardware and software, whose purpose is to collect, process, store, route and present data.[23]

XIII.2.FIREWALL

A firewall is a network protection device that monitors incoming and outgoing traffic, and decides whether to allow or block some of this traffic based on a set of predefined security rules.[24]

Firewalls have been the first line of defence for networks for over 25 years. They establish a barrier between trusted, secure and controlled internal networks and external networks such as the Internet.

A firewall can be hardware or software, SaaS (software used as a service), or hosted in a public or private (virtual) cloud.

XIII.3.PASSWORD PROTECTION

Password protection is an access control technique that protects important data from hackers by restricting their access to information.

Password protection is one of the most common data security tools available to users. [24][25]

[21] https://www.orientation-pour-tous.fr, consulted on 11/10/2023 at 04h08'
[22] https://www.crowdstrike.fr, consulted on 11/10/2023 at 04h11 '
[23] Jacques LONCHAMP, introduction aux systemes informatiques, Paris, Dunod, 2017, p.1.
[24] https://www.cisco.com, consulted on 11/10/2023 at 04h28'.
[25] https://www.microsoft.com, consulted on 11/10/2023 at 04h41 '

XIII.3.1.WHY IS PASSWORD PROTECTION IMPORTANT?

Passwords are the first line of defence against unauthorised access to devices, files and online accounts. Strong passwords help protect data from malicious people and software. The stronger the password, the more secure the information. Using weak passwords is a bit like leaving the door to your car or house open: it's dangerous.

XIII.3.2.CONSEQUENCES OF WEAK PASSWORDS

Given that the average person has more than 150 online accounts, password fatigue is a reality. It is tempting to use simple passwords or the same password for several accounts rather than creating different passwords for each account. However, password complacency can have devastating consequences for both individual users and businesses.

For individual users, the loss of valuable personal, financial and medical information can have lasting financial and reputational damage. Victims may find themselves unable to buy a car, rent a flat or obtain a mortgage; they may even be denied essential medical services. It often takes time and money to rebuild one's reputation and get one's life back on track.

XIII.4.ANTIVIRUS SOFTWARE

Its name says it all. In computing, an antivirus is a programme designed to protect the machine or device on which it is installed.

Protecting against malicious software. Like the firewall, the antivirus is one of the main security devices for protecting user data and ensuring optimal browsing on the web. This software eliminates or reduces the risk of cyber attacks on computers, phones and tablets with Internet access.

If your computer is attacked by a virus, it can affect it in the following ways

. Slowing down the computer
. Damaging or deleting files
. Hard disk reformatting
. Frequent computer breakdowns

- Loss of data
- Inability to perform a task on the computer or on the Internet[26]

[26] https://geekflare.com, consulted on 11/10/2023 at 04h56'.

CHAPTER XIV

EXCEL FUNCTIONS

XIV .1.COPYING A FORMULA

To copy a formula, proceed as follows:

1. Select the cell containing the formula to be copied into adjacent cells.
2. Place the cursor in the bottom right-hand corner until it changes to a plus sign (+), like this:

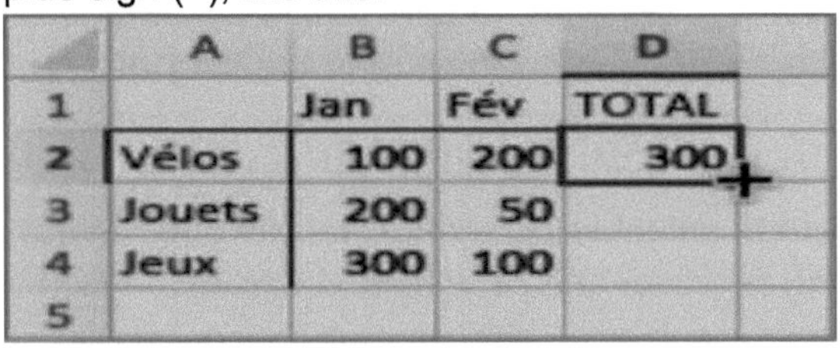

3. Drag the copy handle downwards, upwards or over the cells you want to fill. In this example, the figure below shows how to drag the fill handle downwards:

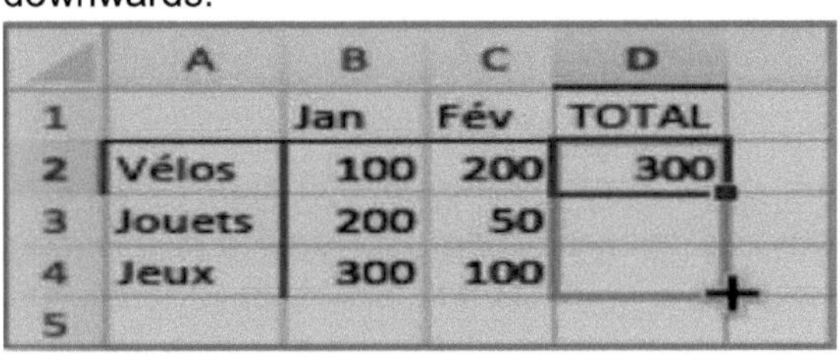

4. When you release your click, the formula is applied automatically to the other cells :

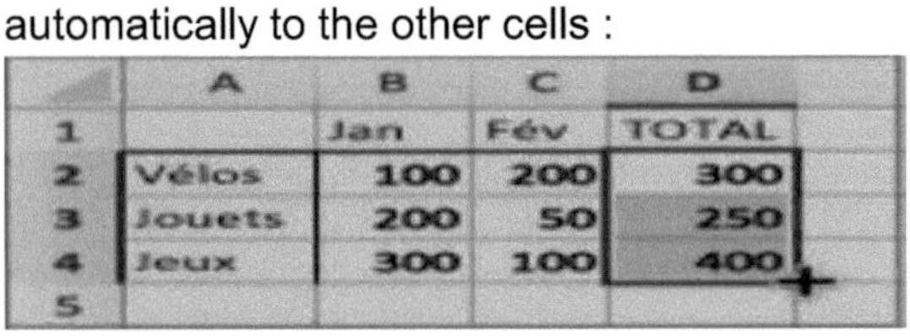

5. To change the copy mode, click on the **Incremental Copy Options** button which appears when you have finished copying, and then on the option of your choice.

XIV.2.NBVL FUNCTION

The Excel **NBVAL** function is used to determine the number of cells that are not empty.

=NBVAL(cell_range)

Example

The aim here is to obtain the total number of members who have made a donation:

	A	B	C
1	Membres	Don(s)	
2	Prénom 1	50.00 €	
3	Prénom 2	111.00 €	
4	Prénom 3		
5	Prénom 4	150.00 €	
6	Prénom 5		
7	Prénom 6	5.00 €	
8	Prénom 7	36.00 €	
9	Prénom 8		
10	Prénom 9	710.00 €	
11	Prénom 10	21.00 €	
12			
13	Nombre de membres ayant fait un don :		
14			

Select the NBVAL function, then simply enter the range of cells in which the number of non-empty cells is to be counted:

=NBVAL(B2:B11)

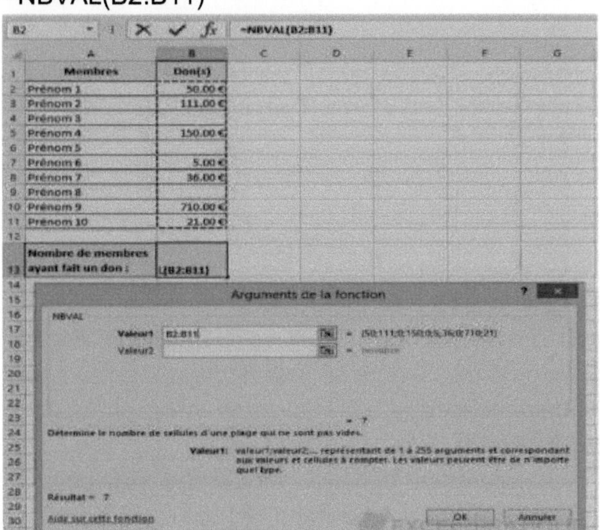

Click on OK to obtain the result:

B13 | =NBVAL(B2:B11)

	A	B	C	D
1	Membres	Don(s)		
2	Prénom 1	50.00 €		
3	Prénom 2	111.00 €		
4	Prénom 3			
5	Prénom 4	150.00 €		
6	Prénom 5			
7	Prénom 6	5.00 €		
8	Prénom 7	36.00 €		
9	Prénom 8			
10	Prénom 9	710.00 €		
11	Prénom 10	21.00 €		
12				
13	Nombre de membres ayant fait un don :	7		
14				

XIV.3.MIN and MAX FUNCTION[27][27]

The MAX function is used to obtain the maximum value of a set of numbers.

=MAX(*number* **)** *"number"* is a reference to a set of numbers or a sequence of numbers separated by semicolons (;).

XIV.3.1.THE MIN FUNCTION

The MIN function is used to obtain the minimum value of a set of numbers.

=MIN(*number* **)**

number" is a reference to a set of numbers or a sequence of numbers separated by semicolons (;).

Example

	A	B	C	D	E	F	Résultat	Formule
1	5	6	8	2	47	3	47	=MAX(A1:F2)
2	1	4	7	9	10	14	1	=MIN(A1:F2)

XIV.4.RELATIVE AND ABSOLUTE REFERENCES

The reference of a cell is the code that allows us to identify it: A1, B3, C15, T375, etc. Some people use the word "cell address", but it is the term "reference" that should be used.

XIV.4.1.RELATIVE REFERENCE

A relative reference is a reference that will vary when you copy it. Relative because the cell references are not fixed (A1, B1,).

[27] https://excel.quebec, c������� �e 11/10/2023 � 12h35�

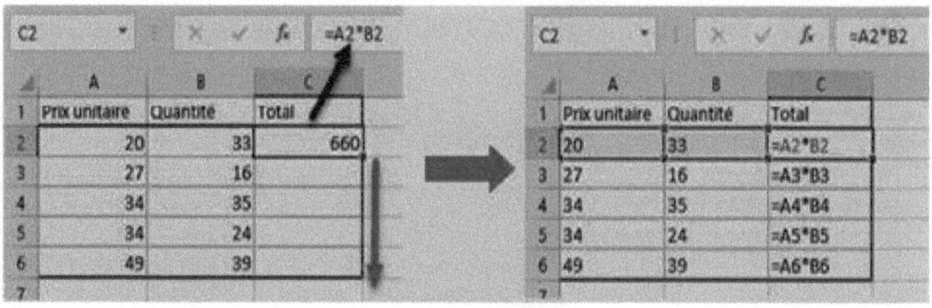

XIV.4.2.ABSOLUTE REFERENCE

An absolute reference is one that will not be modified during a recopy phase. A cell is fixed when you put $ on either side of the reference:

=$F$2

$F$2

To position the two $ in the cell reference, simply press the F4 key on your keyboard.

F4

Example / Mistakes not to be made

To understand the value of an absolute reference, we're going to calculate the price of our sales including VAT. The VAT rate is in cell F1.

ERROR WHEN COPYING

The formula for calculating the price of our sales including VAT is as follows:

=E5*F1+E5

By copying this formula down we quickly identify that there is a problem because we have many errors in column F □????????

	A	B	C	D	E	F	G
1					TVA	18%	
2							
3							
4	Produit	Date	Quantité	Prix unitaire	Total	Total TTC	
5	Produit 6	04/07/2016	3	35	105	123,9	=E5*F1*E5
6	Produit 2	05/07/2016	1	26	26	26	=E6*F2*E6
7	Produit 1	05/07/2016	8	28	224	224	=E7*F3*E7
8	Produit 8	07/07/2016	3	62	186	#VALEUR!	=E8*F4*E8
9	Produit 4	09/07/2016	3	60	180	22482	=E9*F5*E9

CORRECTION OF THE ERROR

In this example, it is easy to see that the VAT reference is shifted when the formula is copied downwards.

So, to stay with cell F1, we're going to write our formula as follows:

=E5*$F$1+E5

By copying our formula, we now have correct calculations because all the formulas use cell F1 ????????

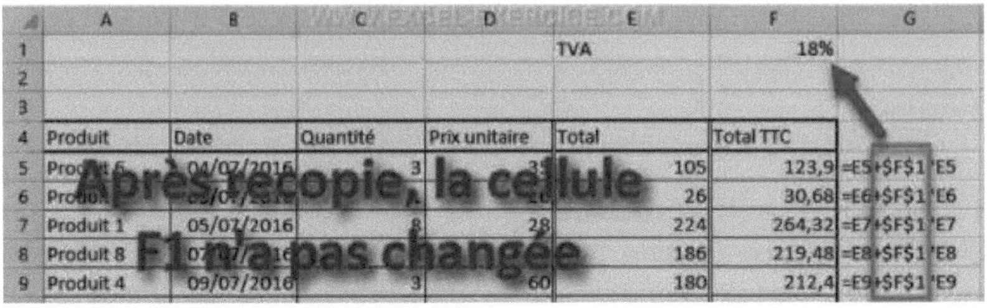

TEST TO CHECK THE FORMULA

Now, if we change the VAT rate to 20%.
. Change the value in F1 to 20%.
Our entire table is updated immediately, taking into account the new data, but the formulas remain the same. ????

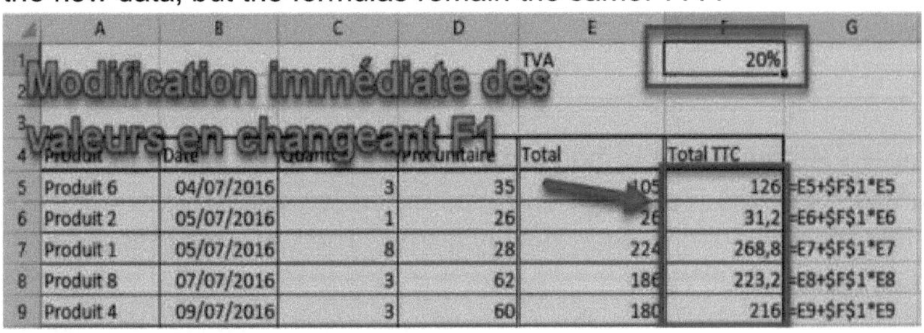

SIMPLIFICATION OF THE FORMULA

You will notice that we use the total reference (column E) twice in the formula. We can simplify this by using the rules for factoring in mathematics, i.e. =E5*(1+$F$1)

BIBLIOGRAPHY

- **The works**
- Curriculum national des Humanites Techniques Commercials, Option: Secretariat-administration.
- Guillaume PLOUIN, *Cloud computing. Securite, gouvernance du SI hybride etpanorama du marché,* 4[e]edition, Dunod, Paris, 2016.
- Jacques LONCHAMP, introduction aux systemes informatiques, Paris, Dunod, 2017.
- **The websites :**
- https://mspoweruser.com
- https://www.inmac-wstore.com
- https://aws.amazon.com
- https://www.phpeasydata.com
- https://www.codyx.org
- https://commentouvrir.com
- https://web.maths.unsw.edu.au
-

More Books!
yes

MIX
Papier aus verantwortungsvollen Quellen
Paper from responsible sources
FSC® C105338

Printed by Books on Demand GmbH, Norderstedt / Germany